Presented to

....

by

....

on

....

Spirit Boosters

FOR THE JOURNEY OF AGING

366 DEVOTIONS

MISSY BUCHANAN

UPPER ROOM BOOKS®
NASHVILLE

Upper Room Books® website: books.upperroom.org

Upper Room®, Upper Room Books®, and design logos are trademarks owned by The Upper Room®, Nashville, Tennessee. All rights reserved.

Cover design: Bruce Gore | Gore Studio, Inc.
Cover photo: Shutterstock

Printed in the United States of America

To Inez Wallace, my childhood Sunday school teacher,
who at 104 is still living each day with purpose
and
to Vista Edmondson, my precious late-in-life friend,
who lives with joy every day in spite of her challenges

New Year's Day is the perfect time to think about how you will approach life in the coming year. Are you creating the legacy you hope to leave one day? What evidence of love and grace trails behind you? Consider your legacy today, and ask God to guide you through the new year.

My only aim is to finish the race and complete the task the Lord Jesus has given me.

—ACTS 20:24 (NIV)

JANUARY 1

Celebrations

....

....

Another year quietly comes to a close. You haven't the energy to party until midnight. Truthfully, you would rather ponder the lessons of the past year. You have learned to choose faith over worry, to choose grace over judgment, to choose humility over pride, and to choose love over hate. These choices will create a lasting legacy of God's faithfulness in your life.

"Choose this day whom you will serve . . . but as for me and my household, we will serve the LORD."

—JOSHUA 24:15

DECEMBER 31

Celebrations

....

....

You need courage to navigate the challenges of aging as questions and worries fill your mind. *What if I fall? Will my living situation change? What if I am unable to care for myself?* Be mindful of examples of God's faithfulness throughout your day. Give thanks, knowing that God will help you make the most of every season of life.

[Jesus] has said, "I will never leave you or forsake you." So we can say with confidence, "The Lord is my helper; I will not be afraid."
—Hebrews 13:5-6

JANUARY 2

Celebrations

When you stare at the lifeless winter landscape, your thoughts turn to the end of life. But below the frozen ground, something is happening. Winter is a time of preparation for the new life that will arrive. You too may be in the winter of your life. Reflect on how you can better prepare to bloom in spring.

Now the winter is past, the rain is over and gone. The flowers appear on the earth; the time of singing has come.

—SONG OF SOLOMON 2:11-12

DECEMBER 30

Celebrations

....

....

As you age, you may be tempted to think you are no longer useful to God. You tell yourself that you are too old, too slow, or too weak. But God has a purpose for you even now. God wants a relationship with you so that you will flourish and bear fruit. Refuse to use your age as an excuse today. Invite the Holy Spirit to show you how to live boldly for God!

In old age they still produce fruit; they are always green and full of sap.
—PSALM 92:14

JANUARY 3

Celebrations

....

....

You may have received a new smartphone for Christmas. You know little about how electronics and the Internet work, but you are amazed at being able to talk face-to-face with a grandchild who lives hundreds of miles away. Give thanks to the God whose abilities soar far beyond all human comprehension.

For as the heavens are higher than the earth, so are my ways higher than your ways and my thoughts than your thoughts.
—Isaiah 55:9

DECEMBER 29

Celebrations
....

....

Another Christmas has come and gone. Packages have been opened and decorations put away. Still, you possess one gift that anyone would love to receive. This gift costs nothing but can change the world one person at a time. The gift is your smile. Give it away freely today.

Our mouth was filled with laughter, and our tongue with shouts of joy.
—PSALM 126:2

JANUARY 4

Celebrations

....

....

You cannot finish life well without intentionally staying focused on God's purpose for your life. Finishing life well demands that you put away selfish pride, and it asks that you make yourself vulnerable. Above all, it takes spiritual strength that comes from first admitting your weaknesses.

If only I may finish my course and the ministry that I received from the Lord Jesus, to testify to the good news of God's grace.
—ACTS 20:24

DECEMBER 28

Celebrations

Think about your oldest possession. Maybe it's a piece of jewelry, a book, a photograph, or a painting. What makes it special is not its monetary value but the story behind it. Ask others to share the story of their oldest possession today. Then, thank God for stories that help you remember who you are.

Remember the days of old, consider the years long past.
—DEUTERONOMY 32:7

JANUARY 5

Celebrations

Remember Shadrach, Meshach, and Abednego? These men are held captive by King Nebuchadnezzar after refusing to bow before a golden idol. They resist the temptation by holding fast to their beliefs. How will you respond when you are tempted in the future?

"Be it known to you, O king, that we will not serve your gods and we will not worship the golden statue that you have set up."

—Daniel 3:18

DECEMBER 27

Celebrations
....

....

At what age did you consider yourself old? There's no transitional moment like when you turned thirteen and became a teenager. Some people are old at fifty; others remain young at 100. Much of aging is determined by your thoughts, so set your mind on God.

Set your minds on things that are above.

—COLOSSIANS 3:2

JANUARY 6

Celebrations

....

....

Think for a moment about the knowledge you have gained over the years. You may be older, but you are still teachable and moldable. Show that you are willing to be a good student. Ask someone to teach you a new skill today.

Give instruction to the wise, and they will become wiser still; teach the righteous and they will gain in learning.

—PROVERBS 9:9

DECEMBER 26

Celebrations

On days when your physical pain is too much to bear, you wonder if anyone understands the burdens you carry. You feel tempted to stay in your bed and close the curtains. But God knows that you need others to help lighten the load. Invite a fellow believer over for coffee and conversation today.

Bear one another's burdens.

—GALATIANS 6:2

JANUARY 7

Celebrations

....

....

There is nothing more beautiful than the faces of loved ones illuminated by candlelight. On this Christmas Day, the light of the Christ child shines brightly. God asks you to reflect that love to everyone you meet. Let your life glow in dark spaces so that others may experience the joy of Christmas.

"I am the light of the world. Whoever follows me will never walk in darkness but will have the light of life."

—JOHN 8:12

DECEMBER 25

Celebrations

Can you recall a time when you lost your temper with a neighbor? Or a time when you chose to watch TV instead of praying or reflecting on God's Word? Do you ever feel as though you lack spiritual discipline? Ask the Holy Spirit to work in you even as you age. Small steps of faith lead to big gains in spiritual growth.

"Blessed are those who hunger and thirst for righteousness, for they will be filled."

—MATTHEW 5:6

JANUARY 8

Celebrations

People encourage you to enjoy life. But that's hard to do when you have nagging pain. God is asking you today to quit waiting for life to get easier or better. The musty stable was not a pristine medical suite. Amidst the messiness of life, the Christ child was born. Christ came to bring you joy in the hardships of the journey.

God did not send his Son into the world to condemn the world, but to save the world through him.

—JOHN 3:17 (NIV)

DECEMBER 24

Celebrations

Don't think for a moment that you have learned all you need to know. You can always gain more knowledge and wisdom. Young people have much to teach you if you are willing to humble yourself. Ask a young person to explain an aspect of technology that you don't understand. Be open and receptive.

"God opposes the proud, but gives grace to the humble."

—James 4:6

JANUARY 9

Celebrations

....

....

You may think that confessing sins is best suited to the season of Lent. But like the innkeeper, sometimes you too turn away the Holy One. Reflect on sins for which you need to repent. Have you been selfish or jealous? Critical or controlling? Repent and receive the gift of forgiveness.

There was no place for [Joseph and Mary] in the inn.
—Luke 2:7

DECEMBER 23

Celebrations

....

....

You watch neighbors and friends walk slowly, pushing their walkers. Their bodies are bent and frail, but, truthfully, they are some of the strongest people you know. Remind yourself that real strength is not a matter of physical ability. Instead, a strong and courageous spirit comes from a relationship with God.

I can do all things through him who strengthens me.

—Philippians 4:13

JANUARY 10

Celebrations

....

....

God is counting on you to share the good news of Jesus' birth. But words alone will not make an impact. Your behavior must reflect your message. If you want to tell others about Jesus bringing hope to a hurting world, then ask yourself if you are living a life of hope. Throughout the day, be a beacon of hope so that others may believe.

May the God of hope fill you with all joy and peace in believing.
—ROMANS 15:13

DECEMBER 22

Celebrations

The late years of life invite you to live with more depth and vulnerability than ever before. For much of your life, you waded in shallow water. You focused more on family, career, and to-do lists than on spiritual maturity. Ponder what it would mean for you to grow in your relationship with God.

Whatever you do, do everything for the glory of God.
—1 CORINTHIANS 10:31

JANUARY 11

Celebrations
....

....

One gift you can give your family members doesn't cost a penny—talking with them about your future. Have you provided clear directives about your wishes for late-life care and funeral arrangements? Do they have access to legal and financial documents? Don't expect them to read your mind. Be proactive and loving.

Do not provoke your children to anger.

—EPHESIANS 6:4

DECEMBER 21

Celebrations

....

....

Consider the advantages of growing older. You no longer have to worry about sucking in your stomach to look thinner. You receive senior discounts at the grocery store and at restaurants. Look on the bright side of life today, and think of at least five positive aspects of growing older.

You shall rise before the aged, and defer to the old; and you shall fear your God.

—LEVITICUS 19:32

JANUARY 12

Celebrations

The embers of a winter fire remind you of your long life. For years, you flamed high with energy, giving off warmth and comfort to others. You blazed until nothing was left but smoldering embers. Invite the Holy Spirit to blow across your life. May your embers kindle a flame for younger generations.

Rekindle the gift of God that is within you . . . for God did not give us a spirit of cowardice, but rather a spirit of power and of love and of self-discipline.

—2 TIMOTHY 1:6-7

DECEMBER 20

Celebrations

Jesus understands the need for healthy boundaries. When the crowds press in around him, he withdraws to be alone with God. Do you ever feel as though others have little regard for your privacy? Consider how you can create boundaries that protect both your privacy and your well-being.

Many crowds would gather to hear [Jesus] and to be cured of their diseases. But he would withdraw to deserted places and pray.
—LUKE 5:15-16

JANUARY 13

Celebrations

Day by day, you feel more vulnerable as your physical body loses its strength. Don't forget that Jesus came to earth to share your humanity and vulnerability. Jesus was exposed and uncomfortable. He too experienced pain and suffering. God loved you so much that God became flesh. Give God the glory!

The Word became flesh and lived among us.

—JOHN 1:14

DECEMBER 19

Celebrations

Every year, people spend billions of dollars on anti-aging products and services in search of the fountain of youth. But nothing can turn back the hands of time. Remind yourself of this truth: The real fountain of youth is found in the joy that comes from a relationship with God.

"The joy of the LORD is your strength."

—NEHEMIAH 8:10

JANUARY 14

Celebrations

....

....

The winter blues have crept in like a thick fog. Though Christmas lights twinkle, all is not so merry and bright in your heart. You feel isolated and alone. You know others who are struggling too. Be the one who brings people together today. Knit scarves for the homeless. Write cards for the hospitalized. Serve others in love.

"By this everyone will know that you are my disciples, if you have love for one another."

—JOHN 13:35

DECEMBER 18

Celebrations

....

....

Remember the story of Queen Esther whose people are to be annihilated? Her cousin Mordecai tells her that she was born for such a time as this; in other words, it is her destiny to save her people. Like Esther, you too were put on this earth for a purpose. Ask God to grant you the wisdom to seek a purpose-filled life in your later years.

"Perhaps you have come to royal dignity for just such a time as this."

—ESTHER 4:14

JANUARY 15

Celebrations

....

....

Remember the Bible story of friends who lower a paralyzed man on a stretcher through the roof so that Jesus can heal him? Because of the friends' faith, the man is healed. God wants you to be a stretcher-bearer for someone today. Find someone who is struggling with life and needs a friend to get him or her to Jesus.

When Jesus saw [the men's] faith, he said, "Friend, your sins are forgiven you."

—Luke 5:20

DECEMBER 17

Celebrations
....

....

How often do you say something, only later to wish you could take it back? Spiritual maturity involves realizing that many aspects of life do not require your comment. Live out your maturity today. Listen to others carefully. Consider your response thoughtfully before speaking.

"On the day of judgment you will have to give an account for every careless word you utter."

—Matthew 12:36

JANUARY 16

Celebrations

Are you still holding a grudge against someone who hurt you long ago? You say you've tried to forgive, but inwardly you know your efforts were half-hearted. Place your grudge at the feet of Jesus today. Pray for release from the resentment and for peace.

First be reconciled to your brother, and then come and offer your gift.
—MATTHEW 5:24 (ESV)

DECEMBER 16

Celebrations

....

....

The world looks different than when you were young, and such change may cause angst and frustration. When you find yourself wanting to criticize youth and modern culture, think about the uncertainty and fears you faced as a young person. How can you offer compassion to young people today? A humble spirit builds bridges between generations.

When pride comes, then comes disgrace; but wisdom is with the humble.
—Proverbs 11:2

JANUARY 17

Celebrations
....

....

In the past, you were always eager for Christmas to arrive. Now that you are older, that sense of anticipation has faded. Perhaps you have confused the miracle in the manger with the excitement of opening gifts. Imagine being on the hillside as the shepherds receive the good news. Listen for the angels' singing.

Suddenly there was with the angel a multitude of the heavenly host, praising God and saying, "Glory to God in the highest heaven."
—Luke 2:13-14

DECEMBER 15

Celebrations
....

....

Living a simple life grants you a great sense of freedom as you age. Instead of accumulating material goods, feel empowered by decluttering and downsizing. Allow yourself to live in the present without fretting about the past or future. Take a step toward simplifying your life today.

We can say with confidence, "The Lord is my helper; I will not be afraid. What can anyone do to me?"

—HEBREWS 13:6

JANUARY 18

Celebrations
....

....

In the Christmas narrative, Mary, Joseph, and the shepherds each hear a similar command: Do not be afraid. You need to hear this message too because a world of fast change and uncertainty may frighten you. God wants to reassure you and bring you hope. You already know how the story ends—love wins.

The angel said to [the shepherds], "Do not be afraid; for see—I am bringing you good news of great joy for all the people."

—Luke 2:10

DECEMBER 14

Celebrations

....

....

Often life does not unfold the way you intended. Loved ones die or move away. Health issues arise unexpectedly. Are you fighting changes that are out of your control? Remember that today's challenges are only temporary in God's eternal plan. Whisper a word of thanks for that truth.

This slight momentary affliction is preparing us for an eternal weight of glory beyond all measure.

—2 CORINTHIANS 4:17

JANUARY 19

Celebrations

You are grateful for the holiday traditions in your family. They provide warm memories and connect the generations. Still, traditions sometimes need new life. Don't hold so tightly to old traditions that you squeeze the joy from new experiences. Be flexible and open to different ways of celebration.

"Why do you break the commandment of God for the sake of your tradition?"

—MATTHEW 15:3

DECEMBER 13

Celebrations

....

....

The cold, gray days of winter may cause you anxiety and sadness. You feel like a caged bird yearning to be free. Instead of letting winter discourage you, use it as a time to tend your inner self. Search your surroundings for simple gifts—a favorite hymn, a warm cup of coffee, a crocheted blanket. Praise God and celebrate the ordinary things that soothe your soul.

I will greatly rejoice in the LORD, my whole being shall exult in my God.
—ISAIAH 61:10

JANUARY 20

Celebrations

You enjoy holiday movies with feel-good story lines and happy endings, but you know from experience that Christmas is difficult for those who are grieving the loss of a loved one. Make time for the people in your life who are grieving. Sit with them. Ask them to share a favorite story about their loved one.

"Blessed are those who mourn, for they will be comforted."
—Matthew 5:4

DECEMBER 12

Celebrations

You have reached the stage in your life when you have far more years behind you than ahead. This sobering thought brings with it a sense of urgency. Don't wait to reconcile with a family member or friend. Be brave. Do something today to mend a broken relationship.

Live in peace; and the God of love and peace will be with you.
—2 CORINTHIANS 13:11

JANUARY 21

Celebrations

....

....

Wherever you are, whatever your age, God can use you to further God's plan. In the story of Jesus' birth, Mary is just a teenager. But Elizabeth, Zechariah, Simeon, and Anna are all quite old. Consider how God can use you right now. Surrender your will to God, and give thanks for the gift of age.

Present your bodies as a living sacrifice, holy and acceptable to God, which is your spiritual worship.

—Romans 12:1

DECEMBER 11

Celebrations

....

....

As a child, you learned the story of Zacchaeus—a small-framed tax collector who climbs a tree so that he can see Jesus above the crowd. How can your life be the tree from which someone gets a better view of Jesus? How do you need to live differently so that others can see Jesus in you?

"The Son of Man came to seek out and to save the lost."

—LUKE 19:10

JANUARY 22

Celebrations

You look forward to holiday gatherings with your family, but you also dread them. The noise level and constant motion overwhelm you. Speak honestly with your loved ones, and help them understand your feelings of vulnerability. Be the loving family that God intends you to be.

A threefold cord is not quickly broken.
—ECCLESIASTES 4:12

DECEMBER 10

Celebrations
....

....

As you've aged, you've probably become more concerned about your blood pressure. It's either too high or too low. Although physical wellness is important, you should also care about your spiritual heart. Start a spiritual exercise regime today to strengthen your heart for God. Stop what you're doing once every hour today and talk to God.

Train yourself in godliness, for, while physical training is of some value, godliness is valuable in every way.

—1 TIMOTHY 4:7-8

JANUARY 23

Celebrations
....

....

Every day you see commercials for anti-aging products that promise to make you look and feel younger. In reality, nothing can stop the aging process. You cannot turn back the hands of time. Instead, God wants you to learn the importance of making each day count. Don't waste this day.

Teach us to count our days that we may gain a wise heart.
—PSALM 90:12

DECEMBER 9

Celebrations

Instead of retreating to a recliner and letting the days pass you by, you have the opportunity to cast a new vision for your later years. God wants to use you for God's glory in spite of your physical challenges. Remember that God cares more about your obedience and faithfulness than your physical abilities.

"If you love me, you will keep my commandments."

—John 14:15

JANUARY 24

Celebrations

....

....

Christmas songs fill the air. But carols about the Christ child are drowned out by silly songs of reindeer and chipmunks. Take time today to clear away the distractions. Turn off the TV and focus on the journey to the manger. Imagine how you might have responded if the angel Gabriel had appeared to you.

In the sixth month the angel Gabriel was sent by God to a town in Galilee called Nazareth, to a virgin engaged to a man whose name was Joseph.
—LUKE 1:26-27

DECEMBER 8

Celebrations

....

....

Sometimes life's problems are overwhelming. The rent for your senior apartment is going up. Another medical test is required. Your prescription still hasn't arrived. Instead of focusing on the negative, keep your eyes on the One who will not fail you. If you only look at your problems, that's all you will ever see. Look up and see God.

"It is the LORD who goes before you. He will be with you; he will not fail you or forsake you. Do not fear or be dismayed."

—DEUTERONOMY 31:8

JANUARY 25

Celebrations

Nature has a way of ushering you into the next season, even when you are not ready. Aging is much the same. You may feel that you are not prepared to enter a new season of life, but it comes anyway. Think about how you will accept the coming season with grace and wisdom.

Be careful then how you live, not as unwise people but as wise, making the most of the time.

—Ephesians 5:15-16

DECEMBER 7

Celebrations

....

....

God has trusted you with the gift of words. Words can wound and break hearts, or they can encourage and heal. You get to decide how you will use the power entrusted to you. Choose words today that will glorify God and give life to others.

Death and life are in the power of the tongue.
—Proverbs 18:21

JANUARY 26

Celebrations

....

....

Today your earthly body feels like a crumbling ruin. Everything is falling apart. On days like this, you fear what the future may hold. Find comfort in knowing that God can replace physical loss with spiritual gain. Trust God to give you wisdom and strength even as your earthly body falters.

"Unless a grain of wheat falls into the earth and dies, it remains just a single grain; but if it dies, it bears much fruit.

—JOHN 12:24

DECEMBER 6

Celebrations

God understands that the aging process is fraught with fears and uncertainties. In fact, people in the Bible often hear this encouraging reminder: Do not be afraid. Remember that God has promised to travel with you every step of your journey. Let your faith be greater than your fear today.

Do not fear, for I am with you, do not be afraid, for I am your God.
—Isaiah 41:10

JANUARY 27

Celebrations

Once upon a time, December was a busy month for you. But now that you are older, you have fewer commitments and less shopping and decorating to do. Instead of shopping, wrapping, and trimming, you have time to savor the significance of Advent. Read the Nativity story once again, and prepare your heart for Christ's coming.

In those days a decree went out from Emperor Augustus that all the world should be registered.

—LUKE 2:1

DECEMBER 5

Celebrations

....

....

The journey of aging takes you through a rugged landscape filled with obstacles—the death of a spouse or friend, medical issues, a move from a house to a nursing facility. Still, you are called to endure and thrive faithfully. Live with confidence today, knowing that when you walk closely with God, hard times will give way to wisdom and strength.

The testing of your faith produces endurance; and let endurance have its full effect, so that you may be mature and complete.

—JAMES 1:3-4

JANUARY 28

Celebrations

With the Christmas season comes the wonderful scents of fresh pine, cinnamon, and apple cider. In contrast, the stable where Jesus was born probably smelled of burning oil lamps and manure. But it also contained the sweet fragrance of a newborn baby. Look for ways to be the aroma of Christ today.

We are the aroma of Christ to God . . . .
—2 CORINTHIANS 2:15

DECEMBER 4

Celebrations

....

....

Winter seems so stubborn, unwilling to release its frigid grasp. You are weary of the weather and the lifeless scene outside your window. Remember that God is still at work in the wintertime. Wrap yourself in the warmth of God's promise to bring new life, and then wait with great expectation.

"I am making all things new."

—REVELATION 21:5

JANUARY 29

Celebrations

....

....

Advent is a time of waiting, and you know how difficult waiting can be. Waiting in the checkout line at the grocery store drains you of energy. Waiting in a doctor's office exhausts you. Yet before Jesus was born, God's people waited hundreds of years for the Messiah. In light of eternity, your wait time on earth is minimal.

*Wait for the L*ORD*, and keep to his way.*

—PSALM 37:34

DECEMBER 3

Celebrations

....

....

Never in its history has the American population been so old. Thanks to medical advances, people live longer than ever before. Still, it can be challenging to grow older in a world that values youth over age. Remind yourself that God intends your later years to be a crowning time of life. Stay close with God and live boldly.

Gray hair is a crown of glory; it is gained in a righteous life.
—PROVERBS 16:31

JANUARY 30

Celebrations
....

....

Over the years you have whittled down your Christmas decorations to just a few boxes. But this year you don't have the energy to get them out. Humble yourself and ask a younger person to help you decorate. Use the time to share stories about Christmases past and your faith.

"God opposes the proud, but gives grace to the humble."

—JAMES 4:6

DECEMBER 2

Celebrations

You thought that by the time you reached your later years, you would have outlived the need to cry. You were wrong. Some days bring deep sadness, grief, or pain. Let your tears be your prayer. Let them flow, knowing that God weeps with you.

I am weary with my moaning; every night I flood my bed with tears; I drench my couch with my weeping.

—Psalm 6:6

JANUARY 31

Celebrations

As you turn the calendar to the last month of the year, remember this: How you finish the year is more important than how you started it. Take this opportunity to reflect on your spiritual growth this year. How have you become more Christlike? Strive to walk as Jesus walked today and every day.

Whoever says, "I abide in him," ought to walk just as he walked.
—1 JOHN 2:6

DECEMBER 1

Celebrations
....

....

At your age, you may struggle with feeling vulnerable. You are not as strong physically as you once were. If you lose your balance and fall, you may land in the hospital. Like a jar of clay, you are fragile and easily shattered. But the treasure inside you is eternal. Give thanks to God for that truth.

We have this treasure in clay jars, so that it may be made clear that this extraordinary power belongs to God and does not come from us.
—2 CORINTHIANS 4:7

FEBRUARY 1

Celebrations
....

....

The year's end is just a few weeks away, prompting you to reflect on the cycle of life. Admittedly, your mind drifts to thoughts about death and dying. Consider what it means to live joyfully in the face of dying. Remember that your journey is not yet complete.

The one who endures to the end will be saved.

—MATTHEW 24:13

NOVEMBER 30

Celebrations
....

....

Today is Groundhog Day, when the world watches to see if a groundhog in Pennsylvania will be frightened by his shadow. Sometimes you too feel frightened by your own shadow. Recall moments when your feelings of uncertainty overcame you. Name your fears aloud, and ask God to conquer them.

Do not fear, for I am with you.

—ISAIAH 41:10

FEBRUARY 2

Celebrations
....

....

In a group of your peers, conversation often turns to the good ol' days. Truthfully, you wouldn't want to sacrifice some of the modern conveniences of today to go back in time. Seek comfort in fond remembrances, but don't try to live in the past. Reflect on the blessings of the present and your hopes for the future.

The Son of God has come and has given us understanding so that we may know him who is true.

—1 John 5:20

NOVEMBER 29

Celebrations

When you were a child, people in their forties seemed old. Today, people in their forties seem young. Your perspective on aging has changed. Remind yourself that God designed you to age. God has ordained purpose for you from birth until death. How will you honor your Creator today?

You shall rise before the aged, and defer to the old; and you shall fear your God.

—LEVITICUS 19:32

FEBRUARY 3

Celebrations

One of the gifts of aging is a heightened awareness of life's simple
blessings. The beauty of a polished apple. The aroma of a pie
baking in the oven. A child's face reflected in candlelight. These
are gifts of exquisite grace. Savor the quiet moments of grace today
and offer thanks.

Bless the LORD, O my soul, and all that is within me, bless his holy name.
—PSALM 103:1

NOVEMBER 28

Celebrations

....

....

At your age, you wonder why it's so hard to talk about your faith. You have a unique opportunity to share how God has worked in your life over many years. Make yourself available to others, and God will use your witness. Step out of your comfort zone, and trust God to work through you.

"Go therefore and make disciples of all nations."

—Matthew 28:19

FEBRUARY 4

Celebrations

You say you believe in the power of prayer, yet you shy away from praying. You have heard the beautiful prayers of others and think your words are too simple, too common. Think again. God is not interested in fancy rhetoric; God is interested in your heart. Share your heart with God today.

This is the boldness we have in him, that if we ask anything according to his will, he hears us.

—1 JOHN 5:14

NOVEMBER 27

Celebrations

Years ago, you embraced your God-given talents and gifts. But now that you have grown older, those gifts seem things of the past. Maybe you can't do what you once did, but you can use your gifts in new ways. Cultivate your unique talents to serve someone today.

Do not neglect the gift that is in you.

—1 TIMOTHY 4:14

FEBRUARY 5

Celebrations
....

....

Some days are especially unforgettable—a milestone celebration, an unexpected tragedy, a long-awaited event. Other days are ordinary, filled with the usual routine. Growing older has taught you to embrace the fullness of life's bounty. Ask God to help you live each day more faithfully.

"I came that they may have life, and have it abundantly."
—JOHN 10:10

NOVEMBER 26

Celebrations
....

....

Family relationships can become complicated as you age because you and your adult children are defining new roles. Remember that God has placed people in your life who want to help you navigate the journey of aging. Be humble when listening to others. Commit to honest, prayerful conversation.

"I give you a new commandment, that you love one another. Just as I have loved you, you also should love one another."

—JOHN 13:34

FEBRUARY 6

Celebrations

....

....

Every day you have the opportunity to encourage someone who is struggling on the journey of aging. God has provided you grace enough to ignite hope in a person who desperately needs it. Who will you reach out to today? Be the spark that shows God's love.

The LORD takes pleasure in those who fear him, in those who hope in his steadfast love.

—PSALM 147:11

NOVEMBER 25

Celebrations

....

....

Do you have an unmet need that constantly nags you? Maybe it's a deeply guarded fear, an important decision to be made, or a broken relationship. Cry out to Jesus. Be persistent in prayer and don't give up. Remember that Jesus hears those who call his name.

"Son of David, have mercy on me!" Jesus stood still and said, "Call him here."

—MARK 10:48-49

FEBRUARY 7

Celebrations

During the holidays, your thoughts turn to family members and the tie that binds you together. In reality, some relationships may be distant and strained. As you gather with family this year, share a little-known story of your ancestors. Sing a favorite hymn. Start a new family tradition. Ask God to be the tie that binds.

Fathers, do not provoke your children to anger, but bring them up in the discipline and instruction of the Lord.

—EPHESIANS 6:4

NOVEMBER 24

Celebrations

Do you look at your life and think that your best years are behind you? God sees it differently. You cannot finish well if you have already moved to the sidelines. Consider what actions you need to take to stand firm in your faith and finish life well. Start with a commitment to focus on God. Something good lies ahead!

. . . fixing our eyes on Jesus, the pioneer and perfecter of faith.
HEBREWS 12:2 (NIV)

FEBRUARY 8

Celebrations

....

....

In this season of life, you recognize the need to live more simply. You have pared down your living space. You surround yourself with less stuff. Now as you prepare to give thanks for your blessings, remember that simplicity gives birth to a season of abundance.

Every generous act of giving, with every perfect gift, is from above.
—JAMES 1:17

NOVEMBER 23

Celebrations

No one enjoys suffering or facing difficult times. But instead of throwing yourself a pity party or isolating yourself in your room, scripture says that comforting another person will bring you comfort as well. Find someone today who needs God's comfort in a time of trial. Do something to show this person God's love.

Praise be to . . . the God of all comfort, who comforts us in all our troubles, so that we can comfort those in any trouble.
—2 CORINTHIANS 1:3-4 (NIV)

FEBRUARY 9

Celebrations

Everybody's got something—some difficulty or struggle of which others may not be aware. An impatient mother has a child with cancer. A grumpy grandfather just moved away from his home of sixty years. Ask God to fill your heart with compassion so that grace will be your response.

If any think they are religious, and do not bridle their tongues but deceive their hearts, their religion is worthless.

—JAMES 1:26

NOVEMBER 22

Celebrations

....

....

The world often pits younger and older generations against each other. But God wants you to interact with and learn from other generations. Reach out to someone who is at least half your age today. Ask him or her to share a favorite Valentine's Day memory. Show that you are interested in what he or she has to say.

In humility value others above yourselves, not looking to your own interests but each of you to the interests of the others.

—PHILIPPIANS 2:3-4 (NIV)

FEBRUARY 10

Celebrations

The world has easy access to knowledge. With digital technology, the answer to almost any question is available in seconds. But facts and figures are not the same as godly wisdom. In spite of having so much knowledge, the world is desperate for wisdom. Ask God to give you wisdom in all circumstances.

God's foolishness is wiser than human wisdom, and God's weakness is stronger than human strength.

—1 CORINTHIANS 1:25

NOVEMBER 21

Celebrations

....

....

Is there someone in your life who annoys you? A person whose behavior just grates on your nerves and makes you want to run and hide? How does God want you to respond to this person? When you next encounter him or her, ask God to help you see beyond that person's faults. Let love direct your response.

[Love] bears all things, believes all things, hopes all things, endures all things.

—1 CORINTHIANS 13:7

FEBRUARY 11

Celebrations
....

....

The holiday season is a mixed bag of emotions. You find joy in the memories of past celebrations, but the season brings sadness because loved ones have passed away. Use old photos of loved ones and their special mementos to decorate a table for the holidays. Let it be an act of love and celebration.

We love because [God] first loved us.

—1 JOHN 4:19

NOVEMBER 20

Celebrations

....

....

Your past holds a key to how you can help others today. How have you suffered or struggled in the past? No doubt you know someone going through a similar crisis. Don't go to him or her with lengthy advice or platitudes. Instead, acknowledge his or her suffering by offering a listening ear and a warm embrace.

Do not neglect to do good and to share what you have, for such sacrifices are pleasing to God.

—HEBREWS 13:16

FEBRUARY 12

Celebrations

Some days the twenty-four-hour news cycle offers nothing but doom and gloom. All the bad news wears you down. Turn off the TV today, and look for God at work in the world around you. Focus on ordinary people doing good deeds and helping others.

"In this world you will have trouble. But take heart! I have overcome the world."

—JOHN 16:33 (NIV)

NOVEMBER 19

Celebrations

Valentine's Day commercials may try to convince you that a giant teddy bear or a dozen roses is the best way to show love. But scripture tells a different story. You show your love for God by following Jesus' commands. How will you love God with all your heart, soul, and mind and your neighbor as yourself today?

"If you love me, you will keep my commandments."

—JOHN 14:15

FEBRUARY 13

Celebrations

....

....

Sometimes you wonder if God really has a plan for your late life. You are physically unable to go on mission trips or teach children's Sunday school like you once did. Be confident in the knowledge that God will give you all you need to live out your faith regardless of your age.

"How much more will your Father in heaven give good things to those who ask him!"

—MATTHEW 7:11

NOVEMBER 18

Celebrations

At this stage of life, you understand that love goes deeper than the romantic words found in a valentine. Offer yourself as God's valentine to a lonely and hurting world today. Let others see God's love through your actions so that they may find hope.

"By this everyone will know that you are my disciples, if you have love for one another."

—JOHN 13:35

FEBRUARY 14

Celebrations

On difficult days, you see growing older as a burden that you must bear. You forget that it can bless you with fresh perspective, rich relationships, and deeper understanding. Ask yourself today what you have learned and are learning from your long life. How would you explain the meaning of life to a twenty-year-old?

"You shall love the Lord your God with all your heart, and with all your soul, and with all your strength, and with all your mind; and your neighbor as yourself."

—Luke 10:27

NOVEMBER 17

Celebrations

....

....

Winter is a stubborn season, seemingly unwilling to let go of its cold grip on the world. But God has planted a seed of hope in your heart. You can be confident that spring will come again because you have witnessed its arrival in years past. Lift up your thanks to the One who is faithful and who brings new life.

May the God of hope fill you with all joy and peace in believing.
—ROMANS 15:13

FEBRUARY 15

Celebrations
....

....

If only young people could automatically download the hard-earned wisdom you've obtained through the years. But you can't force younger generations to accept what you have to offer. Remember that the path to sharing wisdom starts with a pair of ears—yours. Listen first and speak second.

[Make] your ear attentive to wisdom and [incline] your heart to understanding.

—Proverbs 2:2

NOVEMBER 16

Celebrations

....

....

Only now that you no longer have to set an alarm clock for an early workday do you have trouble sleeping past the early hours of the morning. Without sleep, you are prone to irritability. Sleep is God's way of replenishing you. Consider how you can get more sleep. Do you need more physical activity? Less TV before bedtime? Ask your doctor for practical tips for sleeping well.

I will both lie down and sleep in peace.

—Psalm 4:8

FEBRUARY 16

Celebrations

The days are growing shorter. By midafternoon, shadows begin to creep in. Darkness plays with your mind, making it more difficult to be positive about life. Sit quietly in the twilight hour today, and trust the Light of the world. There is no need for despair because Christ is wherever you are.

"I am the light of the world. Whoever follows me will never walk in darkness but will have the light of life."

—John 8:12

NOVEMBER 15

Celebrations

As an older adult, you have a responsibility to younger people. They are watching and learning about aging from you. Think of what you are teaching them about God's faithfulness. Reflect on your responsibility to younger generations and the lessons you are passing on. Are you teaching them well?

We will tell to the coming generation the glorious deeds of the LORD.
—PSALM 78:4

FEBRUARY 17

Celebrations
....

....

Some days you feel like a nobody. People pass by without a word or a glance in your direction. You receive no phone calls, no mail, and no visits. Even so, never forget that you are special to your Creator. God loves you. Christ died for you. The Spirit is within you. Live today like the child of God that you are.

"God so loved the world that he gave his only Son, so that everyone who believes in him may not perish but may have eternal life."

—JOHN 3:16

NOVEMBER 14

Celebrations

In your mind's eye, picture the different telephones you have used over the years. How the designs have changed! Life is all about adapting to change. But now that you are older, change can feel overwhelming. Ask God to help you deal with the changes that come with aging.

*"Be strong and courageous; do not be frightened or dismayed, for the L*ORD *your God is with you wherever you go."*

—JOSHUA 1:9

FEBRUARY 18

Celebrations

You have reached a unique vantage point at this stage of your life, and you can look out over the landscape to see where you have journeyed through the years. Reflect on the perspective you have gained from living such a long time. What can you see that younger people cannot?

[The Lord] leads me in right paths for his name's sake.
—Psalm 23:3

NOVEMBER 13

Celebrations

....

....

Have you experienced disappointment recently? Perhaps a grandchild came to town but didn't stop for a visit. Maybe an old friend moved away to be near her family. Don't allow disappointment to taint your belief in God's goodness. God is faithful, and God loves you. Cling to these blessed assurances, and sing praises to God.

Why are you cast down, O my soul, and why are you disquieted within me? Hope in God; for I shall again praise him, my help and my God.

—PSALM 42:11

FEBRUARY 19

Celebrations
....

....

A church in an active 55+ community has captured its purpose in six words: *Play hard, pray hard, finish well.* Consider your life today with those words in mind. Do you play and pray hard? What might you need to change about your life to find joy in your relationship with God and others? How can you finish well?

I do not run aimlessly, nor do I box as though beating the air.
—1 CORINTHIANS 9:26

NOVEMBER 12

Celebrations

....

....

When it comes to aging, don't compare yourself to others. If you see a ninety-year-old running a half-marathon, feel inspired to exercise more, but don't belittle yourself because you use a cane. Everyone experiences the journey of aging a little differently. Know that God has blessed and will continue to bless your unique journey.

All must test their own work; then that work, rather than their neighbor's work, will become a cause for pride.

—GALATIANS 6:4

FEBRUARY 20

Celebrations

Every day you wake up hoping to have more energy than you had the day before. Rediscover the paradox of aging: The more you work to give yourself away for the benefit of others, the more energized you will feel. Do something special for someone else today.

Do not neglect the gift that is in you.

—1 TIMOTHY 4:14

NOVEMBER 11

Celebrations

Think about the people with whom you interact each day. Are they joyful or bitter, gracious or grouchy? Today you must decide if you will be a positive or negative influence on others. Will you offer joy and compassion or bitterness and cynicism? The choice is yours.

Whatever you do, work at it with all your heart, as working for the Lord, not for human masters.

—Colossians 3:23 (NIV)

FEBRUARY 21

Celebrations

Aging is like a roll of toilet paper. The closer you get to the end, the faster it goes. Do you feel like life is going by faster than ever before? Do calendars and clocks seem unstoppable? Pay attention to each hour of the day and give thanks to God for the gift of time.

With the Lord one day is like a thousand years, and a thousand years are like one day.

—2 Peter 3:8

NOVEMBER 10

Celebrations

Now that you have aged, your energy has waned. You walk more slowly, and daily tasks require more time. Don't be dismayed. Those who rush often miss the miracles of new life. Think of the daffodil that slowly pushes its way through the lifeless ground. Slowing down invites you to celebrate the wonders of life.

You are the God who works wonders; you have displayed your might among the peoples.

—PSALM 77:14

FEBRUARY 22

Celebrations
....

....

Do you have a friend who is at least twenty-five years younger than you? Invest time and energy in the life of a younger person today. Instead of being separated by age, be united by your common humanity. Listen to and learn from each other.

One generation shall laud your works to another, and shall declare your mighty acts.

—PSALM 145:4

NOVEMBER 9

Celebrations

....

....

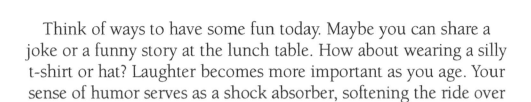

Think of ways to have some fun today. Maybe you can share a joke or a funny story at the lunch table. How about wearing a silly t-shirt or hat? Laughter becomes more important as you age. Your sense of humor serves as a shock absorber, softening the ride over the bumpy ground of life. Help others laugh today.

He will yet fill your mouth with laughter, and your lips with shouts of joy.
—JOB 8:21

FEBRUARY 23

Celebrations

The blazing trees of autumn soon give way to a network of bare branches. As you watch the leaves fall to the ground, remember that some aspects of your life need to fall away too. Perhaps it's your false belief that you can control everything. Maybe it's your resentment or disappointment. Allow these negative thoughts to fall away.

The human mind may devise many plans, but it is the purpose of the Lord *that will be established.*

—Proverbs 19:21

NOVEMBER 8

Celebrations

With thinning hair and orthopedic shoes, you may not feel very holy. But holiness is not about your appearance; instead, it is about pursuing a genuine likeness to your Creator. Today you will be tempted to act in unholy ways. Consider the consequences of your actions, and make an effort to walk in holiness.

God did not call us to impurity but in holiness.
—1 Thessalonians 4:7

FEBRUARY 24

Celebrations
....

....

What you practice today will most likely become your future. If you don't want to become a cranky, miserable ninety-nine-year-old, then practice being humble, kind, and joyful today. Righteousness is yours through faith in Christ.

If you know that he is righteous, you know that everyone who does what is right has been born of him.

—1 John 2:29 (niv)

NOVEMBER 7

Celebrations

....

....

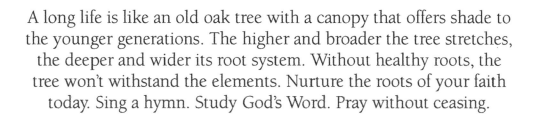

A long life is like an old oak tree with a canopy that offers shade to the younger generations. The higher and broader the tree stretches, the deeper and wider its root system. Without healthy roots, the tree won't withstand the elements. Nurture the roots of your faith today. Sing a hymn. Study God's Word. Pray without ceasing.

"Every good tree bears good fruit."

—Matthew 7:17

FEBRUARY 25

Celebrations

Autumn reminds you that nature waxes and wanes. The leaves that began in spring as small curls of vibrant green are now full-grown with burnished hues and veins that give them shape. As they begin to fall to the ground and crackle underfoot, ponder the cycle of your own life and give thanks.

For everything there is a season, and a time for every matter under heaven.

—Ecclesiastes 3:1

NOVEMBER 6

Celebrations

....

....

As an older adult, you may worry about money more now than you did before retirement. You didn't know how costly it would be to live this long. With every rent increase and medical bill, you worry yourself into a frenzy. Turn your worries into prayers today. Seek wise financial advice, and trust God to show you the way.

"Do not worry about tomorrow, for tomorrow will worry about itself."
—MATTHEW 6:34 (NIV)

FEBRUARY 26

Celebrations
....

....

For years, you helped prepare the Thanksgiving meal, but physically, you just can't do it anymore. Accept your present reality, and focus on the things you can do. Write a Thanksgiving prayer for your family. Share a holiday story from your past. Find a new way to contribute your gifts.

*Give thanks to the L*ORD, *for he is good; for his steadfast love endures forever.*

—1 Chronicles 16:34

NOVEMBER 5

Celebrations

....

....

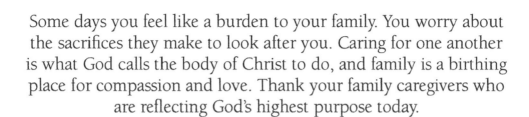

Some days you feel like a burden to your family. You worry about the sacrifices they make to look after you. Caring for one another is what God calls the body of Christ to do, and family is a birthing place for compassion and love. Thank your family caregivers who are reflecting God's highest purpose today.

"This is my commandment, that you love one another as I have loved you."

—JOHN 15:12

FEBRUARY 27

Celebrations

After the Israelites are freed in Egypt, they grumble that their old life as slaves was better than freedom in the desert. You are sometimes deceived into thinking that your earlier life was free from pain and struggle too. It wasn't. Trust in God's guidance, and choose to live faithfully in your current circumstances.

The whole congregation of the Israelites complained . . . .
—Exodus 16:2

NOVEMBER 4

Celebrations

Watching a sports legend on television takes you back to when you were young. Back then, you were fit and active too. Building faith is like building a healthy body. Faith can turn to apathy if it is not exercised and nurtured. Reflect on God's Word, and strengthen your faith today.

You must make every effort to support your faith with goodness, and goodness with knowledge.

—2 PETER 1:5

FEBRUARY 28

Celebrations

This time of year brings allergies, colds, and the flu. One day you begin to feel sick, and your daily activities come to a sudden halt. Illness often brings feelings of sadness and loneliness, but it can also offer time for you to connect with your Creator. Call out to the God who cares for you and hears your cry in times of illness.

Be gracious to me, O LORD, for I am languishing; O LORD, heal me.
—PSALM 6:2

NOVEMBER 3

Celebrations

Leap day—a gift of twenty-four hours that only comes every four years. Picture a child standing anxiously at the edge of a swimming pool, trying to muster the courage to jump into his father's arms. That child is you. What leap of faith will you take to show that you trust God? What is holding you back?

"You of little faith, why did you doubt?"

—Matthew 14:31

FEBRUARY 29

Celebrations

....

....

November is a time to be especially mindful of the blessings in life. Every day from now until Thanksgiving, look for God moments—those times when God speaks to you through an unexpected incident. Look for God's presence in everyone you meet and in everything you do. Give thanks!

Let us come into [God's] presence with thanksgiving.
—Psalm 95:2

NOVEMBER 2

Celebrations

As you age, you feel tempted to focus more on your physical health than on your spiritual health. It's easy to neglect your relationship with God as you deal with medical appointments and prescriptions. Remember that the state of your soul is vital to your well-being. Do something to nourish your soul today.

Beloved, I pray that all may go well with you and that you may be in good health, just as it is well with your soul.

—3 John 2:2

MARCH 1

Celebrations

....

....

On this All Saints' Day, reflect on the godly men and women in your life who have finished their time on earth—family members, friends, teachers, pastors, and neighbors. May their selfless acts of service and dedication to God encourage you to faithfully press on in your own journey.

Since we are surrounded by so great a cloud of witnesses . . . let us run with perseverance the race that is set before us.

—HEBREWS 12:1

NOVEMBER 1

Celebrations

....

....

Some days you feel like a beat-up truck stuck in the mud and spinning its wheels. Because of their unbelief, the Israelites had a similar experience as they wandered in the wilderness for forty years. Ask God to remove any rebellion or unbelief from your heart so that your faith and relationship with God can move forward.

For the Israelites traveled forty years in the wilderness . . . not having listened to the voice of the LORD.

—JOSHUA 5:6

MARCH 2

Celebrations

Children will dress up tonight as pirates, princesses, and superheroes. As darkness comes, jack-o'-lanterns and luminaries will shine on porches and sidewalks. You too can bring light and joy to a dark and weary world. Live your life as a light that shows others the way to Christ.

"Let your light shine before others, so that they may see your good works and give glory to your Father in heaven."

—MATTHEW 5:16

OCTOBER 31

Celebrations

....

....

During the season of Lent, you may decide to give up something as a symbol of the sacrifice Jesus made on the cross. Instead of giving up chocolate or caffeine, what if you gave up harboring a critical spirit? Begin by replacing words of complaint with words of encouragement.

"God so loved the world that he gave his only Son."

—JOHN 3:16

MARCH 3

Celebrations

....

....

After a storm, a thick blanket of damp leaves covers the ground. Until the leaves are raked, you cannot see the walkways. Likewise, aging makes seeing God's path for your life difficult. When faced with questions such as, *Should I stay in my home or move?* or *Should I move to this place or that place?*, trust that God will make your paths known.

Trust in the LORD with all your heart, and do not rely on your own insight. In all your ways acknowledge him, and he will make straight your paths.

—PROVERBS 3:5-6

OCTOBER 30

Celebrations

After a cold, dreary winter, you are anxious to see wildflowers burst forth and bring color to your world. You long for the brown grass to turn green and for the leaves to unfurl on the bare trees. While you wait for spring to arrive, seek joy and beauty in your current situation. Where do you see God working in the world?

My heart is glad, and my soul rejoices.

—Psalm 16:9

MARCH 4

Celebrations

....

....

At your age, you may regularly visit a cardiologist who runs tests on your heart. God, the Great Physician, is even more interested in your heart's condition. While the cardiologist listens for heartbeats and rhythms, God looks for love, humility, and forgiveness. Ask God to guard your heart's health today.

Keep your heart with all vigilance, for from it flow the springs of life.
—PROVERBS 4:23

OCTOBER 29

Celebrations

....

....

Those March winds certainly do howl. You must hold tight to a walker or cane so that you don't lose your balance. One thing you know for certain is that you cannot control the wind. Likewise, the Holy Spirit blows where it will. Be like a wind turbine that utilizes the power of the wind. Ask the Spirit to fill you with energy and new life.

"The wind blows where it chooses . . . but you do not know where it comes from or where it goes. So it is with everyone who is born of the Spirit."

—JOHN 3:8

MARCH 5

Celebrations

....

....

Sometimes you enjoy sifting through old photographs. The images stir your memory of long-ago vacations, birthday parties, weddings, and school events. Reflect today on how God's hands were clearly evident in your life throughout the years. Realizing God's presence in the past will help you trust God in the future.

I will call to mind the deeds of the Lord; I will remember your wonders of old.

—Psalm 77:11

OCTOBER 28

Celebrations

....

....

God gave you specific passions and abilities. Now that you are older, you may worry that you have fewer opportunities to use your gifts. Think again. God wants you to find new ways to utilize your strengths. Be creative. How will you use your gifts today?

We are his workmanship, having been created in Christ Jesus for good works.

—EPHESIANS 2:10 (NET)

MARCH 6

Celebrations

....

....

The unexpected moments of life are like two sides of a coin. You receive glorious news that a grandchild is engaged or that a son is coming home from overseas. Then you hear of a sudden death or diagnosis that brings you to your knees. Know that God will always find a way to create good from the bad.

We know that all things work together for good for those who love God, who are called according to his purpose.

—ROMANS 8:28

OCTOBER 27

Celebrations

Put a single goal in the forefront of your mind today: Be the reason that others smile. Do so by passing along a compliment, sharing a funny story from your childhood, or inviting someone to your home for cookies and tea. Be intentional about smiling, and look for the return on your investment.

Look to him, and be radiant.

—Psalm 34:5

MARCH 7

Celebrations
....

....

In many ways, what you decide to do today can make your tomorrow better. Want to feel God's presence tomorrow morning when you wake up? Read the Bible and pray today. Want to feel happier? Invite a friend to join you for ice cream. Plan today for a better day tomorrow.

Commit your work to the Lord, and your plans will be established.
—Proverbs 16:3

OCTOBER 26

Celebrations

....

....

Do you ever look around and wonder how so much clutter has accumulated since you last decluttered? You've had every intention of throwing away those old magazines and newspapers and takeout containers, but here they are. Persevere today by taking action. Enjoy the freedom of cleaning out and throwing away.

All things should be done decently and in order.
—1 CORINTHIANS 14:40

MARCH 8

Celebrations
....

....

An older woman sits in church just a few days after her husband's death. When the congregation begins to sing a favorite hymn, she starts to cry. A friend hugs her and whispers in her ear, "It's OK. I will sing for you until you are able to sing again." Sit with a grieving person today. Be his or her song of hope.

"Blessed are those who mourn, for they will be comforted."
—Matthew 5:4

OCTOBER 25

Celebrations

As spring inches closer, your thoughts may turn to gardening. So much work goes into reaping a bountiful harvest, and the same is true about your spiritual life. Enrich the soil of your life with prayer and reflections on God's Word today, and one day you will reap the benefits of a magnificent harvest.

As for that in the good soil, these are the ones who, when they hear the word, hold it fast in an honest and good heart, and bear fruit with patient endurance.

—LUKE 8:15

MARCH 9

Celebrations
....

....

Set one important goal for today: Make someone feel loved. Whether that person is a child, a teenager, an older neighbor, a service worker, or a stranger in the checkout line, your actions can make a difference. Step out of your comfort zone, and do something unexpected to help another person experience Christ's love.

Beloved, let us love one another, because love is from God.
—1 JOHN 4:7

OCTOBER 24

Celebrations
....

....

What will you pass down to future generations? Cynicism and impatience? Selfishness and grouchiness? Your behavior will shape the younger people in your life. Be mindful of how you act today. Pass along traits like joy, love, and patience.

The fruit of the Spirit is love, joy, peace, patience, kindness, generosity, faithfulness, gentleness, and self-control.

—GALATIANS 5:22-23

MARCH 10

Celebrations

....

....

When you hear a news anchor describe an active sixty-five-year-old as elderly, you shake your head. It reminds you that the world uses confusing labels for aging. Reflect on ways you can embrace the idea of being a spiritual elder. Wear the title proudly as you model a life of respect, dignity, and God-given purpose.

Brothers and sisters, do not be children in your thinking.
—1 CORINTHIANS 14:20

OCTOBER 23

Celebrations

Do you ever feel as though you watch too much television? Do the sounds of cable news, game shows, and comedy reruns fill much of your day? Instead of surfing the channels today, turn off the TV and read your Bible. Saturate your mind with God's Word and prayer. Ask God to bring new insight into your life.

All scripture is inspired by God and is useful for teaching, for reproof, for correction, and for training in righteousness.

—2 TIMOTHY 3:16

MARCH 11

Celebrations

....

....

As younger family members make their own parenting decisions, you may feel tempted to give unsolicited advice. Refrain from chiming in with your opinion unless asked. Even then, choose your words carefully. Remember that wisdom involves knowing when to speak and when to stay silent.

We urge you . . . to aspire to live quietly, to mind your own affairs.
—1 Thessalonians 4:10-11

OCTOBER 22

Celebrations

....

....

Life would be easier if you didn't have to constantly worry about your physical body—arthritis and heart issues, vision and hearing problems. Even so, your body is an amazing gift that has served you well. Give thanks to God, and do everything you can to care for your body.

Do you not know that your body is a temple of the Holy Spirit within you?
—1 Corinthians 6:19

MARCH 12

Celebrations

....

....

Sometimes you question God's love for you as you deal with the physical challenges of aging. When your mind is filled with doubt, seek out the beauty of God's creation. Experience the simple joy of seeing a plump pumpkin on a porch. Feel the warm embrace of a friend or caregiver. Let God's creation remind you of God's love.

I love those who love me, and those who seek me find me.
—PROVERBS 8:17 (NIV)

OCTOBER 21

Celebrations
....

....

When you look back on your life, you remember times when you wandered away from God, times when you thought you had life under control. But then something happened to remind you just how desperately you need a Savior. Return to God's side today, and stay close for the rest of your journey.

Even now, says the LORD, return to me with all your heart.
—JOEL 2:12

MARCH 13

Celebrations

....

....

The leaves are nearing the end of their life cycle. Gold, orange, red, and yellow—they are stunningly beautiful as they shimmer in the morning light. Consider how you too have become more beautiful with age. Through your life experiences, you are more interesting, more colorful, and more knowledgeable. Share these gifts with the world around you.

The beauty of the aged is their gray hair.

—Proverbs 20:29

OCTOBER 20

Celebrations

You may keep a soft blanket to spread over you when you rest on chilly days. It is cozy, warm, and comforting. In the Bible, the Holy Spirit is sometimes called the *Comforter*—that is, someone who lifts you up and gives you courage. As you pull your blanket around your legs or shoulders today, ask the Spirit to bring you comfort.

The Comforter, even the Holy Spirit, whom the Father will send in my name, he shall teach you all things.

—JOHN 14:26 (ASV)

MARCH 14

Celebrations

....

....

Do you go through the day constantly complaining? The lunch service is too slow. The soup is lukewarm. There are mushrooms in the casserole. It's easy to grumble when you feel lifeless. Instead of groaning today, hold your tongue. Say positive, life-giving words to others, and feel joy come back into your life.

Do everything without grumbling or arguing.
—Philippians 2:14 (NIV)

OCTOBER 19

Celebrations

When your friends and family haven't come to visit in a while, you may feel lonely or abandoned. Perhaps they take part in activities you can no longer participate in, and you feel left out. Know that your Heavenly Father has enclosed you in love and is holding you close even now. God is with you always.

You hem me in, behind and before, and lay your hand upon me.
—PSALM 139:5

MARCH 15

Celebrations

....

....

You woke up this morning with a choice to make. Will you be bitter, or will you be better? How you respond is up to you. You can blame God or resent other people for the challenges of life. Or you can choose to praise God in spite of them. Choose the better way today by walking with God.

Get rid of all bitterness, rage and anger, brawling and slander, along with every form of malice.

—EPHESIANS 4:31 (NIV)

OCTOBER 18

Celebrations

The older you get, the harder praying becomes. That's how it seems when the words are slow to come and your mind wanders. Remind yourself that prayer is about aligning your will to God's will. Don't worry about your words; God is more concerned with the contents of your heart. Talk to God, and God will listen.

"When you are praying, do not heap up empty phrases as the Gentiles do; for they think that they will be heard because of their many words."
—Matthew 6:7

MARCH 16

Celebrations
....

....

Consider the characteristics you would most like to see lived out in the people around you. Do you want to receive more kindness and grace? Do you want to see people acting with more respect and integrity? Whenever you wonder what you can contribute to the world, reflect on the change you want to see. Be that change!

Those who have been born into God's family do not make a practice of sinning, because God's life is in them.

—1 JOHN 3:9 (NLT)

OCTOBER 17

Celebrations

....

....

Life is unpredictable. Events transpire—both good and bad—that you never thought possible. Being flexible is the key to living well. Show that you can be steadfast in your faith but adaptable to new situations. Find ways to praise God regardless of your circumstances.

I have learned the secret of being well-fed and of going hungry, of having plenty and of being in need. I can do all things through him who strengthens me.

—PHILIPPIANS 4:12-13

MARCH 17

Celebrations

....

....

Every day you are tempted to gossip about others. You take delight in hearing a story about someone's personal dilemma, and you quickly share the story with a neighbor. Instead of spreading gossip about someone today, whisper a prayer.

Keep your tongue from evil, and your lips from speaking deceit.
—PSALM 34:13

OCTOBER 16

Celebrations

If you try to run a race while looking behind you, you will most likely stumble. Though reflecting upon and learning from the past is important, you must focus on what's ahead. Put your energy into the race that is before you. How can you run toward Jesus today?

Holy brothers and sisters, who share in the heavenly calling, fix your thoughts on Jesus.

—HEBREWS 3:1 (NIV)

MARCH 18

Celebrations
....

....

The journey of aging is a family affair. Every generation in your family—from the older adults to the brand-new babies—has something to offer. Each has something to teach. Like the branches on a tree, family members grow in different directions, but they are anchored by one root system. Pray for your extended family today.

They are like trees planted by streams of water, which yield their fruit in its season.

—PSALM 1:3

OCTOBER 15

Celebrations

....

....

Does the thought of carrying even two grocery bags at a time make your arms feel weary? Remember that the Shepherd's arms never get tired. God will carry you and hold you close whenever the burdens of life wear you down.

He tends his flock like a shepherd: He gathers the lambs in his arms and carries them close to his heart.

—Isaiah 40:11 (NIV)

MARCH 19

Celebrations
....

....

Some days you feel on edge and irritable. Your eyesight is worsening; your hearing is too. The changes of aging are frightening. You worry about doctor visits and what will happen in the future. Turn your worry into prayers today. Don't let fears about tomorrow rob you of today's joy.

Are any among you suffering? They should pray.

—JAMES 5:13

OCTOBER 14

Celebrations

You may find asking for help to be difficult, especially if you've always been an independent person. But at this point in your life, you can't physically do what you once did. Being humble enough to ask for help opens the door for grace to enter. Who will you ask for help today? Who can you help? Seek humility in all you do.

How does God's love abide in anyone who has the world's goods and sees a brother or sister in need and yet refuses help?

—1 JOHN 3:17

MARCH 20

Celebrations

....

....

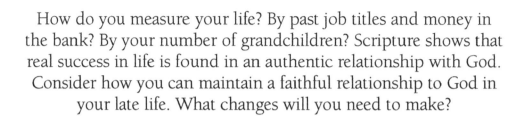

How do you measure your life? By past job titles and money in the bank? By your number of grandchildren? Scripture shows that real success in life is found in an authentic relationship with God. Consider how you can maintain a faithful relationship to God in your late life. What changes will you need to make?

Humble yourselves before the Lord, and he will exalt you.

—James 4:10

OCTOBER 13

Celebrations

....

....

Wisdom does not automatically come with age; it comes from walking closely with God. One mark of the wisdom that only comes from God is knowing when to close your mouth and be silent. As you go through the day, keep that thought in mind. Choose to be wise in all that you say and do.

The tongue of the wise brings healing.

—Proverbs 12:18

MARCH 21

Celebrations
....

....

At your age, your mind naturally wanders into the past. As you contemplate the events of your life, think of the many relationships you have built and the situations you have experienced. Ask God to help you overcome any shame and forgive any guilt that you feel. It is not too late for God to wipe your slate clean.

Repent therefore, and turn to God so that your sins may be wiped out.
—Acts 3:19

OCTOBER 12

Celebrations
....

....

Throughout your life, you've felt the pain of rejection. With each rejection, a callus formed around your tender heart to protect you from more pain. But a tough, callused heart keeps you from accepting and expressing love. Ask God to make your heart tender and soft, able to give and receive love.

Get rid of all bitterness, rage and anger, brawling and slander, along with every form of malice.

—Ephesians 4:31 (NIV)

MARCH 22

Celebrations

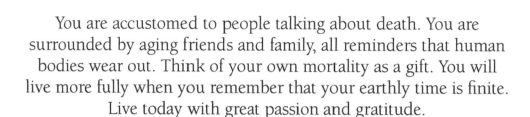

You are accustomed to people talking about death. You are surrounded by aging friends and family, all reminders that human bodies wear out. Think of your own mortality as a gift. You will live more fully when you remember that your earthly time is finite. Live today with great passion and gratitude.

You do not even know what tomorrow will bring. What is your life? For you are a mist that appears for a little while and then vanishes.

—JAMES 4:14

OCTOBER 11

Celebrations

....

....

Some days you wonder if you have the strength to go on—days when life turns you upside down and you are holding on by a thread. Pour out your heart to the God who hears your cries. Be confident in the power of the One who gives you strength to meet a new day.

Why are you cast down, O my soul, and why are you disquieted within me? Hope in God; for I shall again praise him, my help and my God.
—PSALM 42:11

MARCH 23

Celebrations

....

....

Can you still sing the school song from your alma mater? Do you tap your toes when you hear a song on the radio or TV? Give thanks to God for the music in your life. Sing your alma mater. Listen to a radio station that plays music from your high school years. Music will make your spirits soar.

Break forth into joyous song and sing praises.

—PSALM 98:4

OCTOBER 10

Celebrations

....

....

What begins as a grumbling in your heart will likely become a complaint that spews from your mouth. If you allow criticism and anger to well up inside, they will spill out through sharp words. Refrain from stewing in your frustrations today. Ask God to purify your heart and give you a positive outlook.

Let the words of my mouth and the meditation of my heart be acceptable to you, O Lord, my rock and my redeemer.

—Psalm 19:14

MARCH 24

Celebrations

....

....

As you grow older, you value authenticity more and more. The days of trying to prove yourself or live up to a certain image have diminished. Look inside yourself for any remaining pretense. Let your life glow with authenticity so that you can be the person God created you to be.

"The Lord does not look at the things people look at. People look at the outward appearance, but the Lord looks at the heart."

1 Samuel 16:7 (niv)

OCTOBER 9

Celebrations

....

....

You are surrounded by people with broken hearts and broken dreams. Even those who appear to be happy and carefree actually may be desperate to find hope. Offer hope to the people you encounter today. Show acceptance for who they are, and show appreciation for what they do.

The hope of the righteous ends in gladness.

—Proverbs 10:28

MARCH 25

Celebrations

....

....

One glimpse out the window and you are reminded that God is the artist of the seasons. Each magnificent display of nature eventually fades into another season. Consider how you are navigating the transitions of life as you move from one season to the next. Is your life filled with grateful acceptance or bitter resistance?

Godliness with contentment is great gain.
—1 TIMOTHY 6:6 (NIV)

OCTOBER 8

Celebrations

Does thinking about the future make your stomach turn? Growing older holds so many unknowns. Where will you live? What if you get dementia? Soon your concerns grow into fear. Overcome your fear by singing songs of praise today. Repeat favorite hymns until you feel peace and reassurance once again.

*I will sing to the L*ORD *as long as I live; I will sing praise to my God while I have being.*

—PSALM 104:33

MARCH 26

Celebrations

....

....

Are you allowing culture to define aging for you? Do you buy into the hype that you must look and act younger to be valuable? As a believer, you should look at aging differently than the rest of the world. God has given you a purpose regardless of your age. Live joyfully into God's plan.

Even to your old age I am he, even when you turn gray I will carry you. I have made, and I will bear; I will carry and will save.

—Isaiah 46:4

OCTOBER 7

Celebrations

....

....

Somewhere along the way you quit believing that God is for you. With all the challenges of aging, you begin to think that maybe God is punishing you by making life difficult. Instead of despairing, commit to trusting the One who is always loving you, cheering for you, and wanting the best for you.

Surely I know the plans I have for you, says the LORD, plans for your welfare and not for harm, to give you a future with hope.
—JEREMIAH 29:11

MARCH 27

Celebrations
....

....

Do you ever feel as though this season of life is too good to be true? Your career is finished, your children are successfully raised, and your loved ones are nearby. Remember that your relationship with God needs tending in good times too. Don't wait until bad times come to reach out to God. Praise God for the goodness of life.

You will seek the Lord your God, and you will find him if you search after him with all your heart and soul.

—Deuteronomy 4:29

OCTOBER 6

Celebrations

....

....

God wants to help you on the journey of aging. God encourages you to seek God as you make important decisions. God wants you to move forward in faith and not run away in fear. Express your concerns and worries to God today, and allow God to lead you safely into the unknown.

I will instruct you and teach you the way you should go; I will counsel you with my eye upon you.

—PSALM 32:8

MARCH 28

Celebrations

....

....

If you live in a senior community, you likely speak hundreds—if not thousands—of words in a day. With little thought, you talk to neighbors and staff persons, family and strangers. Ask yourself today if your words reflect God's glory. Are your words kind, encouraging, and grace-filled? Pay attention and choose your words wisely.

Those who guard their mouths preserve their lives; those who open wide their lips come to ruin.

—Proverbs 13:3

OCTOBER 5

Celebrations

....

....

Even after all these years, you feel woefully inadequate when compared to the image of Christ. You are still a sinner. You gossip and complain. You forget to love your neighbor as yourself. At times you are prideful and resist a life of prayer. Confess your sins today. God will forgive you and help you grow into the likeness of Christ.

. . . be conformed to the image of his Son.

—ROMANS 8:29

MARCH 29

Celebrations

....

....

You had hoped that when you reached late life you would no longer be stressed. Think again. Stress from medical appointments, health setbacks, prideful people, and changing schedules nags at you daily. Give special care to your soul today. Center your mind on Christ, and repeat the scripture below.

"Seek first his kingdom and his righteousness, and all these things will be given to you as well."

—Matthew 6:33 (niv)

OCTOBER 4

Celebrations

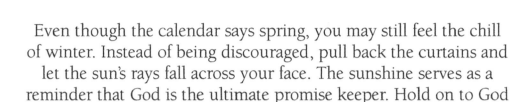

Even though the calendar says spring, you may still feel the chill of winter. Instead of being discouraged, pull back the curtains and let the sun's rays fall across your face. The sunshine serves as a reminder that God is the ultimate promise keeper. Hold on to God and believe. Good days are ahead.

The LORD is trustworthy in all he promises and faithful in all he does.
—PSALM 145:13 (NIV)

MARCH 30

Celebrations
....

....

In this late season of life, you feel a quiet stirring in your soul. Each new day brings you closer to death, and you realize just how precious life is. Spend time today thinking about how you might create a legacy of hope and faithfulness.

Bless the LORD, O my soul, and all that is within me, bless his holy name.
—PSALM 103:1

OCTOBER 3

Celebrations

....

....

To be wise is to know what to overlook—a friend who is always late, a neighbor who talks too loud, a grandchild who would rather text than talk face-to-face. Frustrating and rude? Perhaps. Instead of becoming angry, remind yourself that God's grace is enough to transform your irritations into a smile.

"My grace is sufficient for you, for my power is made perfect in weakness."
—2 Corinthians 12:9

MARCH 31

Celebrations
....

....

When was the last time someone hurt you with sharp words? In that moment, perhaps you wanted to reply angrily in retaliation, but something prompted you to stop. A spiritually mature person tries to understand the reason behind another's wounded spirit and mean words. Strive for maturity today as you interact with others who have troubles of their own.

"If anyone strikes you on the right cheek, turn the other also."
—MATTHEW 5:39

OCTOBER 2

Celebrations

Today is April Fool's Day, and people like to play practical jokes on one another. You want to believe you are too wise and too old to be duped. But in reality, when you listen to the world and disobey God, you are being foolish. Train yourself to listen for God's voice. Live honorably—not foolishly.

Honor is not fitting for a fool.

—Proverbs 26:1

APRIL 1

Celebrations

....

....

The phrase *golden years* takes its cue from an autumn landscape of tall grasses and leaves gilded in gold. Fall is the season of comfort—cozy fires, red apples, and plaid blankets. Think about aging in the context of a glorious autumn afternoon. What do you value most about your current age?

"Where your treasure is, there your heart will be also."
—Matthew 6:21

OCTOBER 1

Celebrations
....

....

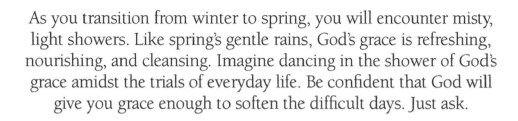

As you transition from winter to spring, you will encounter misty, light showers. Like spring's gentle rains, God's grace is refreshing, nourishing, and cleansing. Imagine dancing in the shower of God's grace amidst the trials of everyday life. Be confident that God will give you grace enough to soften the difficult days. Just ask.

I will send down the showers in their season; they shall be showers of blessing.

—EZEKIEL 34:26

APRIL 2

Celebrations

As you age, life doesn't become easier or less worrisome. But it can become more interesting and more meaningful. Today you have the opportunity to invest your time and energy in the lives of younger loved ones to help them grow and flourish. Be a model of faithful living.

Rise up and tell [the teachings] to their children, so that they should set their hope in God.

—Psalm 78:6-7

SEPTEMBER 30

Celebrations

....

....

You are a child of God. You were created in God's image with a purpose and a calling that is uniquely yours. The same is true for the teenager with a nose ring and tattoo-covered arms. Do not look down on anyone who is different than you. Be humble as you encounter others today. Offer grace, not judgment.

All who are led by the Spirit of God are children of God.
—ROMANS 8:14

APRIL 3

Celebrations

....

....

Learning to lean on God alone is difficult for someone as independent as you. You have always been self-reliant, but you are learning that you can't do everything on your own. Leaning on God is more than just saying you believe in God. Submit totally to the One who is your refuge and strength.

God is our refuge and strength, a very present help in trouble.
—Psalm 46:1

SEPTEMBER 29

Celebrations

....

....

In the journey of aging, you yearn for simplicity. But living a simple life in a complex world is not easy. Living a simple life means focusing on what really matters. Consider how you spend your time today. Are you focusing on what matters most? What priorities need to change?

"If any want to become my followers, let them deny themselves and take up their cross daily and follow me."

—LUKE 9:23

APRIL 4

Celebrations

You want to be happy as you grow older, but true happiness only flows out of a relationship with God. If you seek happiness instead of God, you will be disappointed. Seek a renewed relationship with God, and discover the gift of happiness.

Happy are those who keep his decrees, who seek him with their whole heart.

—PSALM 119:2

SEPTEMBER 28

Celebrations

Every day you encounter difficult, seemingly unlovable people who challenge your goodwill. As a disciple of Christ, you are called to draw upon God's unending provision of compassion and grace and share it with others. Let your kindness be the good news for someone who desperately needs it today.

"Love your enemies, do good to those who hate you, bless those who curse you, pray for those who abuse you."

—LUKE 6:27-28

APRIL 5

Celebrations

....

....

You wonder how people can say there is no God. Do they think the changing seasons are only a scientific phenomenon? Do they not stand and gape at the migrating geese or the beautiful symmetry of a monarch butterfly? Be in awe of the Creator's handiwork, and give thanks today.

They speak of the glorious splendor of your majesty—and I will meditate on your wonderful works.

—Psalm 145:5 (NIV)

SEPTEMBER 27

Celebrations

....

....

At this point in your life, you probably think you've outgrown idol worship. You have little interest in TV celebrities or material goods. Remember, however, that an idol is anything that takes the place of God. Do you worship the god of youthfulness? Are you clinging to days long past? Praise the only One worthy of your worship today.

Their idols are silver and gold, the work of human hands.

—PSALM 115:4

APRIL 6

Celebrations

....

....

You have emotional scars to show for your long life. Some were from self-inflicted wounds, others were caused by people you love, and a few were the result of circumstances beyond your control. Don't confuse scars with failure. Scars show that you have lived! Ask God to turn your scars into stories of hope.

Since, then, we have such a hope, we act with great boldness.
—2 CORINTHIANS 3:12

SEPTEMBER 26

Celebrations

Do you ever feel as though you can no longer help others? Maybe you feel limited by your physical or financial situation. But God is calling you to think anew. No act of service is too small. Look for an opportunity to help someone else today. Hold a door. Give a hug. Share a book. Do something.

Each of you should use whatever gift you have received to serve others.
—1 PETER 4:10 (NIV)

APRIL 7

Celebrations

....

....

Every day you feel tempted to complain about your limitations. Your way of thinking, however, could be limiting you more than any physical ailment. Instead of focusing on your inability to drive to the library to volunteer, read to a neighbor whose vision is diminished. Rethink what you can do, and use your gifts in new ways.

"It is more blessed to give than to receive."

—ACTS 20:35

SEPTEMBER 25

Celebrations

Sometimes life can be difficult. You fear the death of friends and family, a cancer diagnosis, or a long-distance move. You know that God never promised a trouble-free life, but God promises never to forsake you. Be courageous. Look for ways to step outside your fear. God will walk alongside you.

"Be strong and courageous. Do not be afraid; do not be discouraged, for the Lord your God will be with you wherever you go."

—Joshua 1:9 (NIV)

APRIL 8

Celebrations

....

....

As an older adult, God calls you to encourage younger generations. Instead of washing your hands of all responsibilities, use your experience to inspire and engage young leaders. Make a call or write a note today. Do something to let a young person know that you can offer support and wisdom.

Even to old age and gray hairs, O God, do not forsake me, until I proclaim your might to all the generations to come.

—PSALM 71:18

SEPTEMBER 24

Celebrations
....

....

You never intended to be a negative person. But over time, toxic thoughts seeped into your mind and poisoned your disposition. Resentment, pain, and selfish pride hardened into bitterness. Ask God to detoxify your thoughts and cleanse you of all negativity. Say only pleasant words to the people you encounter today.

Keep your heart with all vigilance, for from it flow the springs of life.
—Proverbs 4:23

APRIL 9

Celebrations

When you look back on your life, do you feel as though you already have completed all you were called to do? The answer is simple: No. Your calling is not extinguished just because you have grown older. You will experience life's highest calling when you make sacrifices for others. Think about how you can serve your neighbors today.

Let us love, not in word or speech, but in truth and action.

—1 JOHN 3:18

SEPTEMBER 23

Celebrations
....

....

With age comes worry. Perhaps you worry about broken bones and illness, hospitals and rehab, money and relationships. But worrying will never solve your problems. Instead of providing a way to move forward, worry only saps your strength and energy. When you catch yourself worrying, intentionally give your problems to God.

"Can any of you by worrying add a single hour to your span of life?"
—LUKE 12:25

APRIL 10

Celebrations
....

....

September brings cooler mornings and softer, more mellow sunlight. September's light provides a good way to think about aging. How can you become softer and more mellow as you interact with others today? Look for ways to be warm, congenial, and approachable.

How very good and pleasant it is when kindred live together in unity!
—Psalm 133:1

SEPTEMBER 22

Celebrations

....

....

Spring is the season of resurrection. After the dead of winter, the grass is greening, trees are leafing, and flowers are blooming. Thank God for painting this magnificent picture of the redemption story in nature. Breathe deeply. Feel your heartbeat. Experience renewal and hope coming alive in you.

"Everyone who lives and believes in me will never die."
—John 11:26

APRIL 11

Celebrations

When you were younger, you faced the consequences of your bad decisions. Sometimes you became discouraged and wanted to quit. But now that the finish line of your life looms in the distance, God is asking you to keep growing in faith. Instead of giving up, run the full distance of your life with God's help.

Let us run with perseverance the race that is set before us.
—HEBREWS 12:1

SEPTEMBER 21

Celebrations

Sometimes you wake up and think to yourself, *There's no reason for me to get out of bed.* You have no motivation, no anticipation. Each day feels just like the last. Remember that you are called to be a disciple, and discipleship carries no expiration date. Your work on earth is not done. Get up, serve, stretch, and grow!

"If any want to become my followers, let them deny themselves and take up their cross daily and follow me."

—Luke 9:23

APRIL 12

Celebrations

You hear that aging is a gift, but some days you are not so sure. With all the aches and pains and loss of independence, it can feel more like a curse. Reframe how you see aging by thinking of three positive experiences that have come because of your age. When you focus on your blessings, you will find renewed strength.

My flesh and my heart may fail, but God is the strength of my heart and my portion forever.

—Psalm 73:26

SEPTEMBER 20

Celebrations
....

....

Look around you. Do you know another older adult who is struggling with a worn-out body? Someone who is lonely? Someone who needs a big dose of courage? Inspire others through the way you are facing the challenges of aging.

God did not give us a spirit of cowardice, but rather a spirit of power and of love and of self-discipline.

—2 TIMOTHY 1:7

APRIL 13

Celebrations
....

....

Do you ever feel as though you are wasting this stage of your life?
Do you wonder if each new day counts for nothing? Think again.
Even now, God is calling you to live passionately and faithfully.
Show God's glory to others in all you do.

"As long as it is day, we must do the works of him who sent me. Night is coming, when no one can work."

—JOHN 9:4 (NIV)

SEPTEMBER 19

Celebrations

Today's culture often gets its "wisdom" from celebrities or the media. To age well in a culture of superficiality requires wisdom that comes from walking closely with God. When you become aware of the foolish wisdom of the world, look to God's wisdom instead.

The wisdom of this world is foolishness with God.
—1 Corinthians 3:19

APRIL 14

Celebrations
....

....

You may have grown older, but you have not outgrown temptation. Every day you are tempted to gossip or complain. You are tempted to be judgmental or rigid. Whatever the temptation, God can provide you a better alternative. Ask God to help you recognize the temptations in your life and how to overcome them.

When you are tempted, [God] will also provide a way out so that you can endure it.

—1 CORINTHIANS 10:13 (NIV)

SEPTEMBER 18

Celebrations
....

....

Have you ever thought about how you might be shortchanging God? If you are not living in a way that brings God glory, you are robbing God of the recognition that God deserves. Consider your interactions with others and how they may be used for God's glory. May your life reflect God's character today and every day.

Whoever does not love does not know God, for God is love.
—1 JOHN 4:8

APRIL 15

Celebrations

....

....

Have you ever considered that God is waiting on you? While you ask for God to send a neon sign that points to the path you should take in this season of life, God is quietly nudging you toward developing disciplines of daily study, prayer, and exercise. Stop waiting around. Find your direction and move forward.

Train yourself in godliness.

—1 TIMOTHY 4:7

SEPTEMBER 17

Celebrations

Do you ever feel as though God is silent? You cry out into the darkness but hear nothing in return. You feel no nudge, no still small voice in the late hours of night. So how can you know for certain that God is not ignoring you? Pray. Trust. Keep the faith. Wait expectantly with confidence.

After many days the word of the LORD came to Elijah.
—1 KINGS 18:1

APRIL 16

Celebrations

....

....

Someone wronged you years ago, and he or she never apologized. Consequently, you never offered forgiveness, and you still feel disturbed by this. Scripture says that you should forgive just as God forgives you. Confess your sinful attitude today, and ask God to help you be more forgiving.

If we say that we have no sin, we deceive ourselves, and the truth is not in us.

—1 JOHN 1:8

SEPTEMBER 16

Celebrations

....

....

Do you struggle with the idea of *surrender*? The word sounds weak, as if you are giving up. But when you surrender to God, you become stronger. Resist the temptation to try to control everything in life. Surrender yourself to Christ and claim victory today.

Thanks be to God, who gives us the victory through our Lord Jesus Christ.
—1 Corinthians 15:57

APRIL 17

Celebrations
....

....

What are you seeking at this stage of life? Peace and quiet? Happiness and security? Maybe you are just basking in the successes of your past life. As a follower of Christ, you should be seeking ways to be more like him. Think about what you can do to be the hands and feet of Christ in the world. Think about it, and then do it.

Seek the LORD and his strength, seek his presence continually.
—1 CHRONICLES 16:11

SEPTEMBER 15

Celebrations

....

....

A grateful heart is the best companion on the journey of aging. God's Word tells you to be grateful *in* all things, not *for* all things. Even on days when your arthritis acts up or you're feeling emotionally, mentally, and spiritually depleted, you can find blessings all around. Remind yourself to look for God's presence in the details of life and give thanks.

Give thanks in all circumstances; for this is the will of God in Christ Jesus for you.

—1 Thessalonians 5:18

APRIL 18

Celebrations

....

....

You feel torn. You want your adult children to be involved in decisions about your life, but you fear they will take control and leave you out. Consider the important financial and legal information you need to share with them. Be clear about your directives and wishes. Start talking, and make a plan. Don't wait until it's too late!

Without counsel, plans go wrong, but with many advisers they succeed.
—Proverbs 15:22

SEPTEMBER 14

Celebrations

....

....

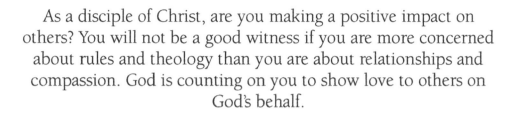

As a disciple of Christ, are you making a positive impact on others? You will not be a good witness if you are more concerned about rules and theology than you are about relationships and compassion. God is counting on you to show love to others on God's behalf.

You were bought with a price; do not become slaves of human masters.
—1 CORINTHIANS 7:23

APRIL 19

Celebrations

....

....

Leaving a longtime home is one of the most difficult things you will ever do. You feel unsettled by letting go of things you worked hard to buy. Remember that your true home is with God in eternity. Embrace the memories of the past but live fully today by keeping an eternal mind-set.

I consider that the sufferings of this present time are not worth comparing with the glory about to be revealed to us.

—ROMANS 8:18

SEPTEMBER 13

Celebrations

....

....

When the days march on in lifeless repetition, the monotony can wear you down. Think for a moment about how God creates a sunrise and sunset every day. Each day begins and ends the same way, and yet every sunrise and sunset holds unique beauty and promise. Ask God to show you the grace and faithfulness of routine.

God called the light Day, and the darkness he called Night. And there was evening and there was morning, the first day.

—GENESIS 1:5

APRIL 20

Celebrations

....

....

You are content living within your comfort zone. At your age, you don't much like risk. But people don't grow and change when they stay in their comfort zone. Take a risk by doing something new and challenging today. Continue to grow spiritually. Instead of saying you can't do something, ask God to show you how you can.

If God is for us, who can be against us?

—ROMANS 8:31 (NIV)

SEPTEMBER 12

Celebrations

....

....

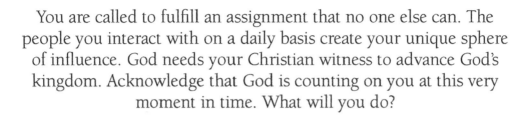

You are called to fulfill an assignment that no one else can. The people you interact with on a daily basis create your unique sphere of influence. God needs your Christian witness to advance God's kingdom. Acknowledge that God is counting on you at this very moment in time. What will you do?

We are what he has made us, created in Christ Jesus for good works.
—EPHESIANS 2:10

APRIL 21

Celebrations
....

....

Have you ever felt as if God were refusing to answer your prayers? Perhaps you gave up too soon. When it comes to life and prayer, your best option is to keep on keeping on. Go to God in prayer today. Then, pray again tomorrow. Don't quit. Keep seeking God.

"Everyone who asks receives; the one who seeks finds; and to the one who knocks, the door will be opened."

—LUKE 11:10 (NIV)

SEPTEMBER 11

Celebrations

Even in your later years, you continue to grow and change. Now is the time for you to flourish in faithfulness and wonder. It is time to grow in understanding, compassion, and wisdom. Celebrate new growth that comes from your relationship with your Creator. Never stop growing!

Grow in the grace and knowledge of our Lord and Savior Jesus Christ.
—2 PETER 3:18

APRIL 22

Celebrations

Once upon a time, you heard God's call. With energy and passion, you responded. Now that you are older, you sometimes wonder if your work is done. But God needs older people too. Consider the Old Testament story of Moses and Aaron and how God uses them in their later years. Be bold, be inspired, and claim your calling!

Moses was eighty years old and Aaron eighty-three when they spoke to Pharaoh.

—Exodus 7:7

SEPTEMBER 10

Celebrations

....

....

Think of times when you have been broken by disappointment, rejection, or loss. Have those times hardened you, or have you allowed God to use the shards of your brokenness to create something beautiful? Humble yourself before God today. Ask your Creator to turn the messes of your life into God's message.

Unless a grain of wheat falls into the earth and dies, it remains just a single grain; but if it dies, it bears much fruit.

—JOHN 12:24

APRIL 23

Celebrations

....

....

You know the grief of losing friends. Some have moved away; others have passed away. You shared wonderful times together, but now they are gone from your life. Cherish your memories, and then focus on nurturing a new friendship with a late-in-life friend. Celebrate the past, but look toward the future.

Above all, clothe yourselves with love, which binds everything together in perfect harmony.

—COLOSSIANS 3:14

SEPTEMBER 9

Celebrations

....

....

Do you ever look back at your life in amazement at how busy you used to be? Somehow you managed many tasks at once. Nowadays you have more unscheduled time but may feel as though you have less to show for it. In reality, time is short. Think of ways that you can invest your time for God today. What will you do?

What is your life? For you are a mist that appears for a little while and then vanishes.

—JAMES 4:14

APRIL 24

Celebrations

....

....

Day by day, year by year, you are called to become more like Christ. This process continues until you take your last breath. Don't think that God is finished with you just because you have grown older. Humble yourself before God, and ask God to make you more like Christ.

Let each of you look not to your own interests, but to the interests of others. Let the same mind be in you that was in Christ Jesus.

—PHILIPPIANS 2:4-5

SEPTEMBER 8

Celebrations

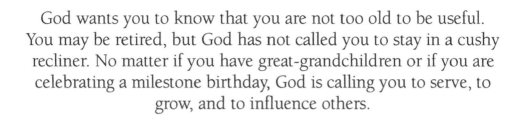

God wants you to know that you are not too old to be useful. You may be retired, but God has not called you to stay in a cushy recliner. No matter if you have great-grandchildren or if you are celebrating a milestone birthday, God is calling you to serve, to grow, and to influence others.

Here I am today, eighty-five years old. I am still as strong today as I was on the day that Moses sent me.

—JOSHUA 14:10-11

APRIL 25

Celebrations

The best epitaph is written while you are still alive. You are shaping your legacy while you are living. Think about what you are engraving on the hearts of others with your words and actions. Is it an epitaph that you hope to leave behind?

We will tell to the coming generation the glorious deeds of the LORD, and his might, and the wonders that he has done.

—PSALM 78:4

SEPTEMBER 7

Celebrations

....

....

Spring is the season when young shoots push up from the ground and tiny leaves open in vivid green. It is a season to commune with the Creator. Take time to smell the sweet fragrance of a new blossom today. Feel the soft breeze on your face. Fellowship with the Creator of the universe and give thanks.

By faith we understand that the universe was formed at God's command.
—HEBREWS 11:3 (NIV)

APRIL 26

Celebrations

....

....

Sometimes you close your eyes and wish you were somewhere else. Perhaps you'd like to be back in your old home or at a favorite vacation spot. Instead of living in a daydream, focus on what you can do right now to make a difference in your current situation. How can you make the best of your present circumstances?

The discerning person looks to wisdom, but the eyes of a fool to the ends of the earth.

—PROVERBS 17:24

SEPTEMBER 6

Celebrations

....

....

Every day you make a choice: Will you grumble, or will you offer praise? Finding a reason to give praise is easy when life is going smoothly. But when life changes unexpectedly, does your praise to turn to grumbling? Ask God to help you keep an attitude of praise even in difficult circumstances.

Do everything without grumbling or arguing, so that you may become blameless and pure.

—PHILIPPIANS 2:14-15 (NIV)

APRIL 27

Celebrations

Moving to a senior living community can be like the first day of school. You wonder if people will like you and if you will make friends. You worry about where you will sit in the dining hall. Celebrate a time when children are going back to school by offering other older adults extravagant hospitality.

Do not neglect to show hospitality to strangers, for by doing that some have entertained angels without knowing it.

—HEBREWS 13:2

SEPTEMBER 5

Celebrations

Now that you are older, you may feel disconnected from the rest of the world. Perhaps you can no longer drive or attend church services. You may feel isolated and alone. Remember that God designed you to be in community with others. Don't try to do life alone. Reach out to someone today who may be feeling lonely too.

Two are better than one, because they have a good reward for their toil. For if they fall, one will lift up the other.

—ECCLESIASTES 4:9-10

APRIL 28

Celebrations

....

....

You push some aspects of aging from your mind so you don't have to think about them. You don't want to consider the possibilities of dementia and long-term care. Be realistic about the parts of aging that require thoughtful planning. Be proactive, and don't procrastinate. Seek the input of your family members and caregivers today.

Commit your work to the LORD, and your plans will be established.
—PROVERBS 16:3

SEPTEMBER 4

Celebrations

....

....

Family members frustrate you when they assume they know what's best for your life. You can tell they get frustrated with you too. Take the initiative today to have an honest conversation with your family about your plans for your journey of aging. Ask for God's grace to cushion your relationship.

Let your speech always be gracious, seasoned with salt, so that you may know how you ought to answer everyone.

—COLOSSIANS 4:6

APRIL 29

Celebrations

....

....

Many times in your past, you thought you could do life on your own. You often relied on your own strength instead of on God's. Know that God wants to help you get through the hardships of today and every day. Trust the only One who gives you renewed strength for the journey.

Trust in the LORD with all your heart and lean not on your own understanding.

—PROVERBS 3:5 (NIV)

SEPTEMBER 3

Celebrations

Jealousy is a temptation of aging. It rears its ugly head when you think someone is getting what you deserve. Perhaps you get upset when a family member chats with your least-favorite neighbor or envy a friend with fewer medical conditions. Don't be jealous. Be grateful for your blessings. Be on guard today against jealousy.

Love is patient, love is kind. It does not envy.
—1 CORINTHIANS 13:4 (NIV)

APRIL 30

Celebrations
....

....

You feel empty but not because you are in need of food. You are hungry for God. Now that getting to church every Sunday is more difficult, you miss being spiritually nourished. Take initiative today by asking others to help you start a small-group study. Give thanks for an increased spiritual appetite that yearns to be fed.

The LORD is good to those who wait for him, to the soul that seeks him.
—LAMENTATIONS 3:25

SEPTEMBER 2

Celebrations

When you share your time and resources with others, you are more likely to feel a sense of hope and purpose. Invite someone for a cup of coffee or send a note to a friend who has moved away. Share a book or a story with another older adult. Give yourself away. Be a blessing and be blessed.

"This is my commandment, that you love one another as I have loved you."

—JOHN 15:12

MAY 1

Celebrations

....

....

Even at this stage of life, you have questions for God. *Why do children get cancer? Why didn't God save you and your loved ones from pain?* You may not receive answers this side of heaven, but God gave you a mind to think and question. Be confident in knowing that God welcomes your questions and honesty.

Now we see in a mirror, dimly, but then we will see face to face. Now I know only in part; then I will know fully, even as I have been fully known.
—1 Corinthians 13:12

SEPTEMBER 1

Celebrations

....

....

As an older adult, you know what it is like to be young, but young people have never been old. Consider how you can share your hard-earned wisdom and life experiences in a way that neither preaches nor condescends. Encourage a young person and make a new relationship.

One generation shall laud your works to another, and shall declare your mighty acts.

—Psalm 145:4

MAY 2

Celebrations
....

....

Keep prayer as your close companion as you make the journey of aging. If you have an unexpected trip to the doctor, pray for courage and strength while you wait. If you find yourself in a painful, broken relationship, ask God for restoration. Whatever your circumstances, lean on God's everlasting arms.

Pray in the Spirit at all times in every prayer and supplication.
—EPHESIANS 6:18

AUGUST 31

Celebrations

....

....

Look at your hands. Instead of focusing on the wrinkles or age spots, reflect on the countless things those hands have done over the years—the meals they prepared, the miles they drove, the hands they held, the people they helped. Celebrate your hands, and think about how you can use them today to be more like Christ.

Moved with compassion, Jesus stretched out His hand and touched him.
—Mark 1:41 (nasb)

MAY 3

Celebrations

As you age, you have an opportunity to savor simple moments in time that younger people often rush through. Savor the aroma of newly mown grass or a cup of freshly brewed coffee. Sit quietly and watch the squirrels and birds as they flit about. Enjoy these moments of grace, and give thanks to God.

Now for a brief moment favor has been shown by the LORD our God.
—EZRA 9:8

AUGUST 30

Celebrations

Popular culture stereotypes older adults as grouchy curmudgeons who like to complain. Chances are you know someone with that kind of critical spirit. God calls you to counter that stereotype. Be a positive influence on everyone you encounter today. Speak kindness, and listen for how your words echo into the world.

The mouths of fools are their ruin, and their lips a snare to themselves.
—Proverbs 18:7

MAY 4

Celebrations

Instead of seeing a senior care community as a waiting room for death, consider it a place to live boldly until your last breath. How can you can reflect God's goodness to others today? Will you give others a high five, a smile, or a hug? Be intentional about living a Spirit-filled life.

God did not give us a spirit of cowardice, but rather a spirit of power and of love and of self-discipline.

—2 TIMOTHY 1:7

AUGUST 29

Celebrations

Good intentions are only that—intentions. Intentions are not actions. Think of something that will encourage another person that you have been intending to do for a long time. Call the friend who is in rehab. Invite the rebellious grandchild to dinner. Write the note of appreciation. Don't wait. Do it today.

"Now that you know these things, you will be blessed if you do them."
—JOHN 13:17 (NIV)

MAY 5

Celebrations
....

....

People seem to want to take advantage of you in your later years. Phone scammers and deceitful companies try to exploit you. Be cautious and wise, but don't become jaded. Most people are not out to get you. Refrain from keeping a cynical outlook, and seek out the good in others.

Be kind to one another, tenderhearted, forgiving one another, as God in Christ has forgiven you.

—EPHESIANS 4:32

AUGUST 28

Celebrations

....

....

Think for a moment about what modern culture values: money, celebrity status, smartphones, and technology. Now think about God's timeless values: humility, compassion, and a pure heart. Make an effort to stay focused on God's values instead of the world's.

The LORD will guide you always.

—ISAIAH 58:11 (NIV)

MAY 6

Celebrations

....

....

Summer seems to have no end. One hot day melts into another until—at last—you feel an autumn chill in the early morning. Like the seasons of the year, aging well requires patience. You want people to be patient with you, but do you extend the same patience to others? Make a point to practice patience in all that you do today.

Rejoice in hope, be patient in suffering, persevere in prayer.
—Romans 12:12

AUGUST 27

Celebrations

Do people sometimes pass by without looking into your eyes? Do family members talk about you as if you cannot hear them? When you feel invisible to the world, remember that God knows you and holds you in high esteem. As you pass by others today, look into their eyes and speak words of affirmation.

The very hairs of your head are all numbered.

—LUKE 12:7 (NIV)

MAY 7

Celebrations

....

....

Looking at your life and recognizing bad habits that have become like heavy chains requires self-awareness. Perhaps you are a couch potato, avoiding all exercise. Maybe you find fault with every person you meet. Create a new, positive habit today. Start by remembering that everyone—yourself included—is a child of God. Look to God for guidance on how to treat yourself and others.

I will meditate on your precepts, and fix my eyes on your ways.
—Psalm 119:15

AUGUST 26

Celebrations

....

....

As you age, remember that your Christian walk does not end in a recliner. Even if you have grown weary or frail, you can still influence others in a mighty way. What one thing will you do today to show God's glory to someone else?

Even though our outer nature is wasting away, our inner nature is being renewed day by day.

—2 CORINTHIANS 4:16

MAY 8

Celebrations

....

....

It's natural to look back over your life and think about mistakes you have made. If only you could undo the hurt you caused others in the past. Remember that your story is not over. It is never too late to ask for forgiveness. Be filled with courage, not regret.

If we confess our sins, he who is faithful and just will forgive us our sins and cleanse us from all unrighteousness.

—1 JOHN 1:9

AUGUST 25

Celebrations
....

....

Remember the gold stars you received in school? They made you feel special and appreciated. Help someone else have a gold-star day. Look for someone who is quietly helping others or who is working hard to fulfill a task. Recognize his or her efforts with words of praise, a hug, or a handwritten note.

Encourage one another and build each other up.
—1 THESSALONIANS 5:11 (NIV)

MAY 9

Celebrations

....

....

All around you, people are criticizing others. Television pundits blast political candidates. Sports stars trash-talk their opponents. Neighbors complain about neighbors. Resolve to go through the day without disparaging another person. Be a joy booster in a critical world.

Do not grumble against one another.

—James 5:9

AUGUST 24

Celebrations

....

....

Too much routine can be dangerous to aging well. How easily you get stuck in a rut! Try eating an unfamiliar food or watching a different TV show today. Read a biography or take up a new hobby. Find an unfamiliar country on a map and research it. Set a goal to try something new every day.

They will still bear fruit in old age, they will stay fresh and green.
—Psalm 92:14 (niv)

MAY 10

Celebrations

....

....

Sometimes God uses an unlikely person to teach you something new. A child shows you how to use a feature on your smartphone. A new neighbor teaches you about life in his country of origin. A teenager introduces you to a new food. Be curious and seek knowledge. Don't quit learning!

An intelligent mind acquires knowledge, and the ear of the wise seeks knowledge.

—Proverbs 18:15

AUGUST 23

Celebrations

You may be old, but you don't have to be cold. Choose to be warmhearted and joyful in spite of your physical challenges. Be intentional about bringing joy to another person today. Share an encouraging quote. Read a story to someone with poor vision. Do something to surprise and warm another's heart.

Rejoice in the Lord always.

—PHILIPPIANS 4:4 (NIV)

MAY 11

Celebrations

Remember when you were a child and you couldn't wait for another birthday? Now you wonder how you got to be so old. Consider the number of years you have lived. Ponder all the changes in technology and transportation that you have embraced throughout the years. Thank God for your own history today!

With long life I will satisfy them, and show them my salvation.

—PSALM 91:16

AUGUST 22

Celebrations

....

....

Laughter acts as a lubricant that makes the day move more smoothly. Tell a favorite joke to friends, or ask others to share a joke of their own. Share a funny story from your childhood, and encourage others to do the same. Be intentional about looking for the bright side of life.

A cheerful heart is good medicine.

—PROVERBS 17:22 (NIV)

MAY 12

Celebrations

....

....

The hot summer sun bears down on your spirit, leaving you parched and dry. Every day you face chronic pain and a sense of uselessness. Remember that God wants to renew your spirit. Draw near to God in prayer today. Sing a favorite hymn. Talk with encouraging friends. Let the cool water of God's grace replenish you.

The LORD will . . . satisfy your needs in parched places, . . . and you shall be like a watered garden, like a spring of water, whose waters never fail.
—ISAIAH 58:11

AUGUST 21

Celebrations

What in your life is a touchstone—a sentimental object that reminds you of a special relationship or memory? It may be your grandmother's rolling pin, an ancestor's Bible, or a letter from long ago. Touchstones hold stories of love. Ask a neighbor or friend to share the story of one of his or her touchstones. Remember that stories bind people together and help them find common ground.

Clothe yourselves with love, which binds everything together in perfect harmony.

—Colossians 3:14

MAY 13

Celebrations

....

....

Now that you are growing older, you find discerning God's will for your life to be difficult. You call out for guidance, but sometimes you feel as though God is not responding. Even when God seems silent, you are called to trust more deeply. Repeat the verse below throughout the day, and have faith that God will act.

*Commit your way to the L*ORD*; trust in him, and he will act.*
—PSALM 37:5

AUGUST 20

Celebrations

....

....

Through the years, your childlike sense of wonder may have diminished. Reignite the curiosity of your inner child by asking *how* and *why* more often. Study the culture of a place you've never visited. Reread a favorite book from your childhood or youth. Stare at the clouds or stars in wonder and awe.

"Truly I tell you, unless you change and become like little children, you will never enter the kingdom of heaven."

—MATTHEW 18:3 (NIV)

MAY 14

Celebrations

....

....

One of the greatest gifts of aging is the accumulation of life lessons. You have gained insight from the school of hard knocks. Now it is time to apply those lessons. Think about what you have learned over the years that will show you how to navigate the future.

Though they fall seven times, they will rise again.
—Proverbs 24:16

AUGUST 19

Celebrations

No doubt you experience days when physical pains nag you or a loved one disappoints you. Soon you feel sad and blue. Before you know it, your entire week starts going downhill. Stop the downward spiral, and accept God's invitation to choose a different color to paint this day. With God's help, you can change your outlook.

"By the tender mercy of our God, the dawn from on high will break upon us."

—LUKE 1:78

MAY 15

Celebrations
....

....

You sit in your favorite recliner and look around. It's sobering to realize that your belongings will one day be sold or given away. But that is your reality. Reflect on traits of great value that cannot be bought or sold—humility, love, compassion, and courage. Act in ways that reflect these priceless characteristics in all you do.

The world and its desire are passing away, but those who do the will of God live forever.

—1 JOHN 2:17

AUGUST 18

Celebrations
....

....

Imagine attending a play where the final curtain comes down after only the first act. You would be disappointed because the story gets more interesting in the second half. Think how fascinating your life is because of the people and circumstances from the second half. Thank God for your long life.

I remember the days of old, I think about all your deeds, I meditate on the works of your hands.

—Psalm 143:5

MAY 16

Celebrations
....

....

God is great. God is good. Let us thank him for our food. How many times have you repeated that simple blessing over the years? Yet God is so much more than great or good; God is your Creator, Redeemer, and friend. The next time you go to pray, think of who God is to you and give thanks.

The one who is in you is greater than the one who is in the world.
—1 JOHN 4:4

AUGUST 17

Celebrations
....

....

Relationships are your most valuable asset. How might you invest in your relationships today? Think about a family member facing failure, loss, or disappointment. Be an encourager, not a judgmental critic. Humble yourself and share with your loved one a time when you were in crisis.

Love one another with mutual affection; outdo one another in showing honor.

—ROMANS 12:10

MAY 17

Celebrations

....

....

You keep a photograph of yourself from decades past. When you look at it, you recall how youthful you once looked, full of energy and promise. Remember that you are called to reflect God's glory at any age. Convey God's likeness instead of your own.

All of us . . . seeing the glory of the Lord as though reflected in a mirror, are being transformed into the same image from one degree of glory to another.

—2 CORINTHIANS 3:18

AUGUST 16

Celebrations

....

....

Be honest with yourself—the realities of aging make you worried and fearful. Maybe you worry about losing your independence, outliving your money, or being diagnosed with dementia. Whatever your fear, you can trust God to care for you. Make more room for God and less room for worry.

Cast all your anxiety on [God], because he cares for you.
—1 PETER 5:7

MAY 18

Celebrations

....

....

Have you ever heard the saying, "Live your life in such a way that the preacher doesn't have to lie at your funeral"? Reflect on your own behavior during the last week. Have you been gracious or grumpy? Encouraging or demanding? Humble or prideful? Live today so that others will be thankful for your life.

I thank my God every time I remember you.

—Philippians 1:3

AUGUST 15

Celebrations

....

....

Every day you face the temptation to make Jesus more like you. From politics to family debates, you are sure that Jesus agrees with your viewpoint. The trouble is, you've got it backward. As a Christian, you are called to be more like Jesus and not the other way around. Be aware of this temptation as you interact with others.

. . . until all of us come to the unity of the faith and of the knowledge of the Son of God, to maturity, to the measure of the full stature of Christ.
—EPHESIANS 4:13

MAY 19

Celebrations
....

....

Some days you feel you have outlived your purpose. You wonder what you can do now that you have physical limitations. Remember that you were created with an important purpose—to glorify God. Be confident in knowing that your life matters. Now it's up to you to make the most of it. What will you do?

"Everyone who is called by my name, whom I created for my glory, whom I formed and made."

—Isaiah 43:7

AUGUST 14

Celebrations

....

....

Some days, even a simple task like making the bed saps your energy. Sometimes you feel as if you are growing weaker day by day. Remember God's wonderful, paradoxical promise: Even if your body grows weak, you can be spiritually strong. Meditate on that thought today. Let God make you strong!

I will strengthen you and help you; I will uphold you with my righteous right hand.

—Isaiah 41:10 (NIV)

MAY 20

Celebrations

....

....

There have been times in your life when you showed great strength by holding fast to something—a goal, a belief, a dream, a relationship. But you have also learned that letting go can be a sign of strength. No matter if you need to hold on or let go, trust God to give you the strength you need today.

Trust in the LORD forever, for in the LORD GOD you have an everlasting rock.
—ISAIAH 26:4

AUGUST 13

Celebrations

Look at your reflection in a mirror when you are not smiling.
Then, flash a grin and notice the difference. There is nothing
more endearing than a smile that has endured tragedy and tears,
heartache and troubles. Give others the best gift ever—your smile.

A cheerful look brings joy to the heart; good news makes for good health.
—Proverbs 15:30 (NLT)

MAY 21

Celebrations
....

....

Yesterday you glanced at a recent photo of yourself. You felt disheartened to see thinning silver hair and a face etched with deep lines. Look at the photo again today. Instead of gray hair, see how deeply you have loved. Instead of wrinkles, see a lifetime of laugher and life experiences. There is beauty in aging.

The beauty of the aged is their gray hair.

—Proverbs 20:29

AUGUST 12

Celebrations

....

....

Gratitude and joy are closely intertwined. When you realize just how blessed you really are—even in the midst of difficult circumstances—you discover a deeper joy. Renew a habit of giving thanks today. Think of three blessings, and, if possible, write them down. Add to the list throughout the week.

O give thanks to the LORD, for he is good; for his steadfast love endures forever.

—PSALM 107:1

MAY 22

Celebrations

On your kitchen table, you see a stack of old magazines and last week's mail. Your closet is stuffed with clothes you no longer wear. The cabinets overflow with trinkets that collect dust. Start the task of clearing your clutter today. Feel the freedom that comes with less stuff and more life.

"Be on your guard against all kinds of greed; for one's life does not consist in the abundance of possessions."

—Luke 12:15

AUGUST 11

Celebrations

....

....

Have you heard the saying "In every apple there is an orchard"?
What kind of legacy are you planting—a legacy of unconditional
love or a legacy of bitterness and pride? You have the potential
to create a bountiful orchard. Sow seeds of faith and love, then
tenderly care for them and watch them grow.

*We will tell to the coming generation the glorious deeds of the LORD, and
his might, and the wonders that he has done.*

—PSALM 78:4

MAY 23

Celebrations

....

....

Over the years, you have learned this important truth: Faith does not guarantee that life will turn out the way you hoped. Even in your later years, life is not fair. But your faith offers another truth: God will never leave or forsake you. Praise God for that!

Give thanks in all circumstances; for this is the will of God in Christ Jesus for you.

—1 THESSALONIANS 5:18

AUGUST 10

Celebrations

Sometimes you feel like you are just a number—a room number, an age, a patient number. But you are God's beloved child who has accumulated decades of life experiences. Celebrate what makes you unique today—your name, your story, your purpose. Rejoice knowing that you belong to God.

I will not forget you. See, I have inscribed you on the palms of my hands.
—Isaiah 49:15-16

MAY 24

Celebrations

....

....

You still remember your childhood—the games you played, your friends and neighbors, your favorite toy—even though it was long ago. Now you are in a new season—elderhood. It is a time of seeking purpose by using your gifts in new ways for the greater good. Show others how to be a godly elder. Don't settle for just being older.

Let the elders who rule well be considered worthy of double honor.
—1 TIMOTHY 5:17

AUGUST 9

Celebrations

....

....

Growing older is more fun if you do it with the right people. Surround yourself with people who are positive, people who lift your spirits, people who laugh easily and often, and people who will encourage you. Then be a person with those traits for the sake of others.

Let us consider how to provoke one another to love and good deeds.
—Hebrews 10:24

MAY 25

Celebrations

....

....

Throughout your life, you have experienced times of tremendous pain—the death of a loved one, a medical diagnosis, or a financial loss. Even now, God can turn your pain into compassion. How can you use the hard lessons of your past to encourage someone today?

Blessed be the God . . . who consoles us in all our affliction, so that we may be able to console those who are in any affliction.

—2 CORINTHIANS 1:3-4

AUGUST 8

Celebrations

....

....

Listening is not only about being silent while someone talks but also about being actively engaged when another person is speaking. Make an effort today to be a great listener. Ask someone to share stories about his or her first job or favorite vacation. Then lean forward and practice the art of listening attentively.

You must understand this, my beloved: let everyone be quick to listen, slow to speak, slow to anger.

—JAMES 1:19

MAY 26

Celebrations

....

....

Take a look at your Bible. Are the pages worn and underlined or stiff from lack of use? Does your Bible stay by your side in times of joy or crisis, or does it sit on a shelf? Don't fool yourself into believing you have outgrown Bible study. Acknowledge your need for the steadfast Word of God, and seek God's wisdom in its pages.

The grass withers, the flower fades; but the word of our God will stand forever.

—Isaiah 40:8

AUGUST 7

Celebrations

....

....

Some say that you cannot fully appreciate the light until you have experienced the darkness. Think of someone you know who is going through a dark season—a time of grief, loss, health crisis, or difficult change. Decide how you will bring light into his or her darkness today.

Let your light shine before others, so that they may see your good works and give glory to your Father in heaven.

—Matthew 5:16

MAY 27

Celebrations
....

....

Reflect on important decisions you made when you were young. When did you feel that you lacked maturity or wisdom? Aging gives you the ability to look back and see your growth over time. Rejoice that God has granted you spiritual growth. Keep growing!

We must no longer be children, tossed to and fro and blown about by every wind of doctrine, by people's trickery, by their craftiness in deceitful scheming.

—EPHESIANS 4:14

AUGUST 6

Celebrations

....

....

Nature is good for your well-being. God calls you to spend time in God's creation. Go outside and breathe in the fresh air. Feel the sunshine across your shoulders. Sit and watch the birds. Praise the works of God's hand, and feel your mood brighten.

[The LORD] makes me lie down in green pastures; he leads me beside still waters.

—PSALM 23:2

MAY 28

Celebrations

....

....

At this stage of life, routine comes easily. In fact, you often get upset if someone disrupts your routine. Challenge this mind-set today. Sit in a different chair at lunch. Skip a favorite TV show, and watch something new. Be flexible! Ask Jesus to bring new life that comes from a relationship with him.

Jesus said to them, "Very truly, I tell you, unless you eat the flesh of the Son of Man and drink his blood, you have no life in you."

—JOHN 6:53

AUGUST 5

Celebrations

The process of aging is constant, even relentless, like the crashing waves. But just like the waves, aging was designed for a purpose by the Creator. You can run from aging, but you cannot stop it. Celebrate the fact that you have survived and thrived for many years. Your long life is a gift that many never receive.

I trust in the steadfast love of God forever and ever.

—Psalm 52:8

MAY 29

Celebrations

....

....

Look past a person's shortcomings to the things he or she does well. Consider a neighbor who is habitually late but never forgets a birthday. Or a man who talks too loud but carves beautiful toys for children. In the light of God's grace, you can banish negativity.

As God's chosen ones, holy and beloved, clothe yourselves with compassion, kindness, humility, meekness, and patience.

—COLOSSIANS 3:12

AUGUST 4

Celebrations

....

....

God did not intend for you to go through life alone. You need other people. Even if you reside in a senior living community, you may feel tempted to isolate yourself. Connect with someone new today. Be brave. Meet a new neighbor. Join a Bible study. Attend a class. Be intentional about living in community.

How very good and pleasant it is when kindred live together in unity!
—Psalm 133:1

MAY 30

Celebrations

....

....

The dog days of summer have arrived, and the oppressive heat can wear you down. Instead of grumbling about the temperature outside, whisper a word of thanks for the sunshine that gives light to the day and life to the flowers and trees. Invite a friend over for a cool drink, and exchange a favorite vacation story.

Offer hospitality to one another without grumbling.
—1 PETER 4:9 (NIV)

AUGUST 3

Celebrations

What would you do if you knew you only had one more day to live? This question will help you focus on what is most important in life. What would you want to say to the people you love? Would you offer words of forgiveness, affirmation, or love? Don't wait. Prepare for tomorrow by living fully today.

Beloved, since God loved us so much, we also ought to love one another.
—1 JOHN 4:11

MAY 31

Celebrations
....

....

When you look at aging through human eyes, you only see loss and pain. God wants to change your perspective on aging and bless and encourage you on your journey. Be mindful today that longevity is part of God's design and something to be cherished.

Abraham breathed his last and died at a good old age, an old man and full of years.

—GENESIS 25:8 (NIV)

AUGUST 2

Celebrations

....

....

Some days you wonder why you are still on this earth. You feel as though you have outlived your purpose, and you mistakenly think that God has forgotten you. God will never overlook you. Glorify the One who first gave you life, and find ways to live into your purpose today.

But this is why I have let you live: to show you my power, and to make my name resound through all the earth.

—Exodus 9:16

JUNE 1

Celebrations

....

....

The late years of life offer you a unique opportunity to make a lasting impression on the lives of others. Whose lives do you most want to impact? What can you do to show God's love to them today? How can you touch them in such a way that they will want to tell the story ten years from now?

Rise up and tell [the teachings] to their children, so that they should set their hope in God.

—Psalm 78:6-7

AUGUST 1

Celebrations

....

....

What is the hardest thing you've ever done? Perhaps you buried a child or went overseas to fight a war. To have lived a long life means that you have persevered through tragedy. Think about how God has brought you through hard times, and give God the glory!

May the God of steadfastness and encouragement grant you to live in harmony with one another, in accordance with Christ Jesus.

—ROMANS 15:5

JUNE 2

Celebrations

....

....

God doesn't use cookie cutters. God made you as a one-of-a-kind. No one on earth is exactly like you. No one shares your particular life experiences. Consider the aspects of your life that make you different from your friends and relatives. Throughout the day, give thanks for God's creativity.

I praise you, for I am fearfully and wonderfully made.

—Psalm 139:14

JULY 31

Celebrations

Music has the ability to lift your spirits, and it is God's gift to you. Add a little music to your life today. Sing in the shower. Listen to hymns or worship songs. Start a senior choir. Ask someone to help you create a playlist of your favorite tunes for a digital device. Don't wait for music to happen. Make your own music and rejoice!

Sing and make music from your heart to the Lord.
—Ephesians 5:19 (NIV)

JUNE 3

Celebrations

....

....

You woke up in a dark reality this morning. Your joints are aching, and your energy is sapped. You are tempted to share your misery with anyone who will listen. Self-pity can become an addiction. Trust God to give you hope and to show you that you are braver and stronger than you think you are.

Why am I discouraged? Why is my heart so sad? I will put my hope in God! I will praise him again—my Savior and my God!

—Psalm 43:5 (NLT)

JULY 30

Celebrations

....

....

When you feel your independence slipping away, you may be tempted to dig in your heels and cling to your old, familiar ways. You need wisdom to discern when to hold onto something and when to let go. Ask God to help you determine God's will, and then move forward in faith.

Do not be conformed to this world, but be transformed by the renewing of your minds, so that you may discern what is the will of God.
—ROMANS 12:2

JUNE 4

Celebrations

....

....

How you speak is just as important as what you say. If you really want others to hear you, use a tone filled with kindness and grace. If you want others to respect you, show them respect. Be the type of person that you would like others to be in return. Never use age as an excuse for bad behavior.

"Do to others as you would have them do to you."

—Luke 6:31

JULY 29

Celebrations

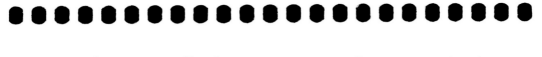

Your later years offer the opportunity to illuminate and to be illuminated. Do not limit what the Holy Spirit can do through you by giving the excuse that you are too old. People of all ages are watching and learning from you. Teach them well. Now is your time to shine!

Let your light shine before others, so that they may see your good works and give glory to your Father in heaven.

—Matthew 5:16

JUNE 5

Celebrations

....

....

Dark clouds gather in the distance. Lightning flashes and thunder rolls as ominous clouds move closer. At your age, you feel especially vulnerable when facing the storms of life. You can no longer run to escape the pounding rain. Lift up your eyes today. Keep them on the Savior and not on the storm.

I keep my eyes always on the LORD. With him at my right hand, I will not be shaken.

—PSALM 16:8 (NIV)

JULY 28

Celebrations

....

....

When you look at your arms, what do you see? Perhaps sagging skin and signs of muscle loss. Your strength has diminished through the years, but God's arms never get weary. They are always open to you. When you picture your relationship with God, imagine yourself running into the strong arms of unconditional love and forgiveness.

[The younger son's] father saw him and was filled with compassion; he ran and put his arms around him and kissed him.

—Luke 15:20

JUNE 6

Celebrations

Some say you are only as old as you feel. On days when your knees buckle and you struggle to get out of your chair, you feel practically ancient. But what if you began your day with a sense of anticipation and wonder instead of anxiety and dread? Start this day in prayer and ask, *God, what great thing are you going to do today?*

"Sanctify yourselves; for tomorrow the LORD *will do wonders among you."*
—JOSHUA 3:5

JULY 27

Celebrations
....

....

The best way to prepare for the uncertainties of tomorrow is to live faithfully today. You are not too old to create a daily habit of prayer and devotional time. Increase your understanding of who God is through study. Then, as you make the journey of aging, you will always be accompanied by hope and faith.

Make me to know your ways, O LORD; teach me your paths.
—PSALM 25:4

JUNE 7

Celebrations
....

....

Do you ever look back on your harsh words or actions and feel the tug of your conscience? As you reflect on recent events, you must admit that you've been quick to criticize and judge others. Confess your sins today, and ask for forgiveness. Your need for repentance does not lessen with age.

All have sinned and fall short of the glory of God.
—ROMANS 3:23

JULY 26

Celebrations

....

....

A woman once said that even though she was growing older, she would never grow old. Her attitude, she explained, made all the difference. You too can keep a fresh outlook on life and resist negativity. Ask God to do a new thing in your life today, even as you continue to age.

See, I am doing a new thing! Now it springs up; do you not perceive it? I am making a way in the wilderness and streams in the wasteland.
—ISAIAH 43:19 (NIV)

JUNE 8

Celebrations
....

....

The image of a stooped body fills you with dread, and the thought of using a walker makes you feel old. Even so, you don't walk as tall as you used to, and you fear falling and breaking a bone. Hold your head high, and remember that you are a treasured child of God whose earthly body is only temporary. Celebrate your identity in Christ.

We know that if the earthly tent we live in is destroyed, we have a building from God, a house not made with hands, eternal in the heavens.

—2 Corinthians 5:1

JULY 25

Celebrations

When your children and grandchildren describe you, what words do you think they use? Words like *kind* and *generous*? Or *judgmental* and *tightfisted*? Decide the words you most want family and friends to use to describe you, and then live in a way that exemplifies those words.

We intend to do what is right not only in the Lord's sight but also in the sight of others.

—2 Corinthians 8:21

JUNE 9

Celebrations

....

....

Every day you interact with people of all ages who have been wounded by life. They struggle with heavy loads of heartache, loss, and disappointment. As an older adult, you have an opportunity to help others heal. Offer mercy and grace to those who are hurting today. Reflect Christ's love.

"My yoke is easy, and my burden is light."

—MATTHEW 11:30

JULY 24

Celebrations

Waiting is hard, even when you feel as if all you have is time. Waiting on a diagnosis or waiting for a family member to visit can be nerve-racking. You may become agitated and discouraged. Memorize John 14:27 today. Write it down, and repeat it anytime you feel overwhelmed by waiting. Never stop asking God to bring you peace.

Peace I leave with you; my peace I give to you. I do not give to you as the world gives. Do not let your hearts be troubled, and do not let them be afraid.

—John 14:27

JUNE 10

Celebrations
....

....

While sitting with a group of friends, your thoughts begin to wander. You ask yourself, *Which one of us will die first?* You aren't afraid of death; instead, what frightens you most is the in-between time. How will your life unfold between this moment and death? Know that your future is in God's hands, and trust in God's promise of eternity.

"For God so loved the world that he gave his only Son, so that everyone who believes in him may not perish but may have eternal life."

—John 3:16

JULY 23

Celebrations
....

....

No matter your physical state, you have a gift to contribute to the world. If you deny or ignore your gift, you rob others of what you have to offer. Maybe it's a high-five or uplifting humor. Maybe it's business expertise or a hobby. Think of a way you can contribute to someone's life today, and then do it.

Serve one another with whatever gift each of you has received.
—1 Peter 4:10

JUNE 11

Celebrations

....

....

You tell yourself that you'll wait until autumn to clear the clutter. You'll wait until the pain is worse before you see the doctor. You'll wait until you hear from a loved one to have that difficult conversation. Stop procrastinating! Take a first step today in dealing with an issue that you've been putting off. Don't delay. Move forward.

Don't put it off; do it now! Don't rest until you do.
—PROVERBS 6:4 (NLT)

JULY 22

Celebrations

....

....

How you deal with the changes in your life says a lot about your spiritual maturity. Do you grumble and complain? Do you blame others when things don't go as you expected? Consider how you have dealt with the changes in your life. Ask God to show you the path to aging faithfully.

Your word is a lamp to my feet and a light to my path.
—Psalm 119:105

JUNE 12

Celebrations
....

....

The journey of aging becomes easier when you accept the realities of life—the ups and downs and in-betweens. Looking back over the years, you can see how even the difficult times made your life richer. Thank God today for taking the hard realities of aging and weaving them into the beautiful artwork that is your life.

We know that all things work together for good for those who love God, who are called according to his purpose.

—ROMANS 8:28

JULY 21

Celebrations

....

....

Young people form opinions about the Christian faith based on their interaction with believers like you. You play the important role of a pointer—someone who points others to Christ. Be mindful of ways you can model a grace-filled life. Let your actions bring glory to God.

Show yourself in all respects a model of good works, and in your teaching show integrity, gravity, and sound speech that cannot be censured.

—TITUS 2:7-8

JUNE 13

Celebrations

....

....

Do you wake up some mornings thinking about your diminishing eyesight? Maybe your strength is waning too. Before you tell yourself that there's little you can do anymore, think again. You have the power to alter the course of someone's day. Reach out to someone you don't know, and make a new friend. Encourage a young person who is struggling. Tap into God's power.

I pray that, according to the riches of his glory, he may grant that you may be strengthened in your inner being with power through his Spirit.

—Ephesians 3:16

JULY 20

Celebrations

God has granted you long life for a reason. Your age is not a mistake or an oversight; it is God's plan. Instead of shrinking away in your later years, choose to embrace your age. Reframe the way you think about aging today. Look at it as an opportunity for serving others and praising God.

I am confident of this, that the one who began a good work among you will bring it to completion by the day of Jesus Christ.

—PHILIPPIANS 1:6

JUNE 14

Celebrations

....

....

Apologizing to someone you've hurt doesn't necessarily get easier with age. But modeling humility keeps you from becoming prideful or rigid. Apologize to someone you may have hurt in the past. Taking the high road in life requires a humble spirit.

Confess your sins to one another, and pray for one another, so that you may be healed.

—JAMES 5:16

JULY 19

Celebrations

....

....

You live in a disposable world where unwanted items are thrown away easily. Sometimes that way of thinking colors how people feel about aging. But that is not God's way; older adults are not disposable. Remember that you are God's valued masterpiece. You are a treasure not to be discarded.

We are God's masterpiece. He has created us anew in Christ Jesus.
—EPHESIANS 2:10 (NLT)

JUNE 15

Celebrations
....

....

Sometimes you feel bogged down by a season of loss. Perhaps you have lost loved ones, your independence, or your belongings. Instead of only considering the negative aspects of loss, think of ways that loss can be positive. What do you gain when you lose feelings of pride, greed, or anger?

Those who want to save their life will lose it, and those who lose their life for my sake, and for the sake of the gospel, will save it.

—MARK 8:35

JULY 18

Celebrations

For good or ill, you will become what you practice every day. Think about negative behaviors you repeat on a regular basis—sarcasm, self-pity, gossip, or selfish pride. Repent and refrain from careless words today. Start a new, positive habit that glorifies God.

Do nothing from selfish ambition or conceit, but in humility regard others as better than yourselves.

—PHILIPPIANS 2:3

JUNE 16

Celebrations

Consider your prayer life. Do you just whisper a quick prayer before meals? Do you only pray when you face an emergency? Give new life to your prayer routine by praying throughout the day. Talk with God about the ordinary and extraordinary parts of everyday life, knowing that God will listen.

"Pray then in this way: Our Father in heaven, hallowed be your name."
—MATTHEW 6:9

JULY 17

Celebrations

Summer brings back childhood memories of going barefoot and chasing fireflies. Wouldn't you love to be that carefree again? Your adult worries of declining physical health or being alone bring you down. Turn over all your worries to the One who cares most for you today. Name your worries one by one.

Cast all your anxiety on [God], because he cares for you.
—1 PETER 5:7

JUNE 17

Celebrations

....

....

Look around for someone who is trying to make your life better. Maybe it's a family member who runs your errands or a staff person who cleans your room. It may be a caregiver, a minister, or a neighbor. Find a way to show appreciation to someone today for what he or she does for you.

Be kind to one another, tenderhearted, forgiving one another, as God in Christ has forgiven you.

—EPHESIANS 4:32

JULY 16

Celebrations

Compare your life to the rock formations of the Grand Canyon. They contain layer upon layer of sediment of different colors and textures, and together they create a work of natural beauty. Your life experiences also have created a magnificent wonder. Live boldly, knowing that you were made to reflect God's faithfulness.

We also boast in our sufferings, knowing that suffering produces endurance, and endurance produces character, and character produces hope.

—Romans 5:3-4

JUNE 18

Celebrations

....

....

Can you pat your head while rubbing your stomach? Like that activity, aging asks that you do two opposite things at once. Aging well requires letting go of some aspects of your life while leaning forward into the unknown at the same time. Think about what you need to release today to move forward.

One thing I do: Forgetting what is behind and straining toward what is ahead.

—Philippians 3:13 (NIV)

JULY 15

Celebrations

....

....

As an aging adult, you have a responsibility to prepare younger family members for the time when your earthly journey is over. Think about what your family members will need after you are gone. A monetary inheritance won't help them nearly as much as a legacy of love that flows from a relationship with God.

Your steadfast love is better than life.

—PSALM 63:3

JUNE 19

Celebrations
....

....

Jesus understands the power of stories. Ask a friend or neighbor to share the story of his or her wedding day. Ask a young person to share his or her favorite summer activity. Be interested in what others have to say. Remember that storytelling binds people of all ages together.

Using the boat as a pulpit, [Jesus] addressed his congregation, telling stories.

—MATTHEW 13:3 (MSG)

JULY 14

Celebrations
....

....

What kind of people do you dread being around? Perhaps you avoid negative people, those whose complaints sap your energy and patience. What sorts of people lift your spirits? Perhaps you feel yourself drawn to those whose enthusiasm and passion for life feels contagious. Commit yourself to being a person who makes others feel glad to be alive.

I have indeed received much joy and encouragement from your love, because the hearts of the saints have been refreshed through you.

—PHILEMON 1:7

JUNE 20

Celebrations

....

....

You yearn for a day of peace and calm—a day with no falls or illness, no phone calls with bad news. But the Bible reminds you that peace is possible in all circumstances. God alone can calm your heart in the midst of suffering. Ask God to grant you peace.

You will keep in perfect peace those whose minds are steadfast, because they trust in you.

—Isaiah 26:3 (NIV)

JULY 13

Celebrations

....

....

As you age, reminiscing about the past and recalling special memories offers comfort. But you set yourself up for disappointment if you try to live in the past. Don't miss what's good about today because you are stuck in yesterday. Live in the confidence that some of your best memories are still to come.

Do not say, "Why were the former days better than these?" For it is not from wisdom that you ask this.

—ECCLESIASTES 7:10

JUNE 21

Celebrations

....

....

Your line of thinking right now can impact the way the rest of your day unfolds. If your mind is flooded with negative news or self-pity, your day's trajectory will be a downward spiral. Be intentional today in filling your mind with uplifting words and images. Guard your heart from negativity.

Keep your heart with all vigilance, for from it flow the springs of life.
—PROVERBS 4:23

JULY 12

Celebrations

....

....

Aging is filled with disruptions: a fall, a health crisis, a move. Unexpected changes can be overwhelming. Your life may not be what you want it to be, but it is your new normal. Ask God to help you accept what you cannot change and to adapt joyfully to your new normal.

The LORD makes firm the steps of the one who delights in him.
—PSALM 37:23 (NIV)

JUNE 22

Celebrations
....

....

People often say that change is a good thing. But in reality, some change is good, and some change isn't. You need wisdom to know the difference. Think about how you determine if a change is good or bad. Are you leaning on God's wisdom to know the difference?

The wisdom from above is first pure, then peaceable, gentle, willing to yield, full of mercy and good fruits, without a trace of partiality or hypocrisy.

—JAMES 3:17

JULY 11

Celebrations

....

....

No doubt you've acquired many material possessions as you've aged. You want to simplify, but how? What can you get rid of? Before you give away beloved treasures, ask a loved one to take photos of the items to save as keepsakes. Then, sort, sell, donate, and throw away. Take a first step to lighten your load.

"Do not store up for yourselves treasures on earth . . . but store up for yourselves treasures in heaven."

—MATTHEW 6:19-20

JUNE 23

Celebrations

....

....

Whatever your age, take pride in the many years you have survived. You have a unique opportunity to take a long view of life, something that young people do not have. Don't try to hide your age. Be grateful for each year and celebrate!

I praise you, for I am fearfully and wonderfully made.
—PSALM 139:14

JULY 10

Celebrations

No one can turn back the hands of time. Instead of trying to recapture your youth, live fully and passionately every day. Don't spend time worrying about your wrinkles and age spots. Instead, embrace your life as it is. What will you do to make your life more interesting and fulfilling?

"I came that they may have life, and have it abundantly."
—JOHN 10:10

JUNE 24

Celebrations

....

....

You grew up in a time when you fixed things that were broken. If something breaks today, people discard it and buy a new one. You aren't surprised that this way of thinking has impacted how people look at aging too. Remember that you are not a throwaway. You are God's treasure.

God proves his love for us in that while we still were sinners Christ died for us.

—ROMANS 5:8

JULY 9

Celebrations
....

....

Many older adults grow apathetic as they age. Their youthful zest for life turns into a don't-care attitude. But others face the challenges of aging with a resilient, quiet courage. Choose the latter today. Don't let apathy steal your joy.

They are darkened in their understanding, alienated from the life of God because of their ignorance and hardness of heart.

—Ephesians 4:18

JUNE 25

Celebrations
....

....

You gaze into a mirror and wonder what happened to the nice-looking twenty-year-old in the wedding photo. Now all you see are sags, wrinkles, and scars. Embrace your changing body with a sense of humor. Don't take yourself too seriously. Every time you pass a mirror, take a look and smile.

Strength and dignity are her clothing, and she laughs at the time to come.
—PROVERBS 31:25

JULY 8

Celebrations
....

....

Sometimes you feel as though young people don't care about what you have to say. Have you ever considered that they fear being judged? Help change their thinking by modeling love and respect. Ask a young adult to share an opinion on something in the news. Be attentive and stop yourself from offering criticism.

Show yourself in all respects a model of good works.

—Titus 2:7

JUNE 26

Celebrations

....

....

Ask yourself the following questions and be honest: Do others enjoy being around you? Do their faces brighten when they see you coming? Or are you feeding the stereotype of a grouchy old person? Evaluate yourself as you interact with others, and look for ways to improve. Be the person God intended you to be.

Welcome one another, therefore, just as Christ has welcomed you, for the glory of God.

—ROMANS 15:7

JULY 7

Celebrations

....

....

Some days you feel lonely, especially if no one has called or dropped by in a while. Everyone is so busy. Even so, it hurts to be overlooked. Give the gift you would most like to receive today: unhurried time. Spend an afternoon with someone who needs a lift. Give yourself away, and be blessed.

Bear one another's burdens, and in this way you will fulfill the law of Christ.

—GALATIANS 6:2

JUNE 27

Celebrations

The journey of aging is not just about making it to your next birthday. And it is more than a biological or psychological phenomenon. For people of faith, aging is lived out in a spiritual dimension. Consider how your faith and wisdom can grow stronger even as your physical body weakens.

"My grace is sufficient for you, for power is made perfect in weakness."
—2 CORINTHIANS 12:9

JULY 6

Celebrations

....

....

What a blessing to be able to look back on years past! You have reached a unique vantage point from which you can observe a long stretch of years. You can see how people's lives intersected at just the right time. You can follow the trail of relationships. Thank God for the blessing of long life.

With long life I will satisfy them, and show them my salvation.
—Psalm 91:16

JUNE 28

Celebrations
....

....

Every day you encounter people whose lives are broken. Think of your life as a billboard that will be seen by others today. How can you use your life to create an inspiring message for others to see? What will your message be?

So shall my word be that goes out from my mouth; it shall not return to me empty, but it shall accomplish that which I purpose, and succeed in the thing for which I sent it.

—Isaiah 55:11

JULY 5

Celebrations
....

....

Have you ever looked at a photo of the sun on the horizon and wondered if it were a sunrise or a sunset? Both views are awe-inspiring. Likewise, birth and death are equally beautiful because you have the promise of eternal life. You can live out your days in peace with the promise of resurrection. Hallelujah!

"I am the resurrection and the life. Those who believe in me, even though they die, will live, and everyone who lives and believes in me will never die."

—JOHN 11:25-26

JUNE 29

Celebrations

On America's Independence Day, think about times when you have felt like a flag twisted by a storm. When it seemed that the winds would blow forever, they suddenly shifted and the flag unfurled. After the storm, you—like the flag—were able to fly freely once again. Take comfort in knowing that hard times do not last. Give God the glory for that truth.

"Call on me in the day of trouble; I will deliver you, and you shall glorify me."

—Psalm 50:15

JULY 4

Celebrations

How are you living out the final chapters in your book of life? What does it mean for you to finish well? Finishing well requires that you take action now. Living faithfully today paves the way for a grace-filled future. How will you serve others and grow spiritually today?

I have fought the good fight, I have finished the race, I have kept the faith. From now on there is reserved for me the crown of righteousness.
—2 TIMOTHY 4:7-8

JUNE 30

Celebrations

....

....

Summertime is the perfect season for reminiscing. This summer, make a commitment to capture your life stories. Write them or record them through video or audio. If you are able to write them yourself, do one story a day. Or ask a loved one to record you telling stories from your life. Don't wait to share your unique history.

Jesus told them a parable about their need to pray always and not to lose heart.

—LUKE 18:1

JULY 3

Celebrations

....

....

You were designed in God's image. That means you possess the same creative spark as the Creator of the universe. When you use your creative gifts, you renew your spirit. Sketch a flower in bloom. Write a poem or a short story. Make up a new verse to an old song. No act is too small. Do whatever you can to celebrate your creative spirit!

God created humankind in his image.

—GENESIS 1:27

JULY 1

Celebrations

Today you will be bombarded with voices of the world— news commentators, celebrities, politicians, commercials—all trying to tell you what is important in life. These clamoring voices will try to drown out God's voice. What can you do today to turn off the chatter and tune in to God?

"Be still, and know that I am God!"

—Psalm 46:10

JULY 2

Celebrations

....

....